Castles and Cathedrals

1066–1500

John Robottom

LONGMAN

Longman Group UK Limited
Longman House, Burnt Mill, Harlow, Essex
CM20 2JE, England and Associated Companies
throughout the World.

First published 1991
Third impression 1992
ISBN 0 582 08250 1

Set in 11/15pt Bodoni (Lasercomp)
Printed in Hong Kong
GC/03

Designed by: Roger Walton Studio
Illustrated by: Andrew Macdonald, Sue Sharples
Cover photograph: Building a castle using spiral
scaffolding, from a fifteenth-century French
manuscript
British Library Royal Ms 15 Dlllf15v

The Publisher's policy is to use paper manufactured from
sustainable forests.

We are grateful to the following for permission to
reproduce photographs:

Aerofilms Ltd, page 57; Airpic, page 77; The
Ancient Art & Architecture Collection, page 69
below; John Bethell Photography, page 16;
Bibliothèque de Dijon, page 53 *below*;
Bibliothèque Nationale, page 31 *above*;
Bibliothèque Royale Albert 1er, page 67; Bodleian
Library, Oxford, pages 27, 45; Ian Booth. By kind
permission of the Dean & Chapter, page 47;
British Library, pages 30, 31 *below*, 33 *left*, 37
below, 38 *above left*, 38 *below*, 51 *below* (photo:
Bridgeman Art Library) 52, 53 *above*, 62, 71
above, 73; British Rail Pension Fund Works of
Art Collection, page 40; Cadw: Welsh Historic
Monuments. Crown Copyright, pages 34, 59
above; The Cathedral Shop, Canterbury
Cathedral, page 15 *above*; The Dean & Chapter of
Durham, page 15 *below*; English Heritage, pages
6, 74; English Life Publications Ltd, Derby, pages
14, 36, 43 *left*, 43 *centre*; The Fotomas Index,
page 78; Giraudon, page 66; Sonia Halliday,
page 70 *above*; Michael Holford, pages 5, 37
above, 50; Angelo Hornak, pages 70 *centre*, 71
below, 72; Museum of London, page 41; National
Library of Wales, page 51 *above*; Pitkin Pictorials,
page 44; Public Record Office: E36/247, page 56;
Royal Commission on Historical Monuments of
England, pages 28, 64, 79 *above*; Crown
Copyright: Royal Commission on the Ancient &
Historical Monuments in Wales, page 8; The
Royal Library, Copenhagen, Denmark, page 69
above; Courtesy of the Marquis of Salisbury,
page 59 *below*; Salisbury & South Wiltshire
Museum, page 10; Skyscan, pages 20 *below*, 24;
Mrs Elizabeth Sorrell, page 9 *above*; Warwick
Castle, page 25; Woodmansterne, pages 9 *below*,
20 *above*, 38 *above right*, 39, 43 *right*, 48, 60, 70
below, 76, 79 *below*, 80; Worthing Museum & Art
Gallery, page 19.

Contents

1 Norman castles and cathedrals

Castles and conquest

In October 1066 William, Duke of Normandy, set sail for England with an army. He believed that he had a better claim to be king of the English than Harold who had become king of England less than a year before. Four or five years later, a monk in the abbey of Jumièges wrote this about William's invasion:

> **1** Thence with a following wind, sails spread aloft, he crossed the sea and landed at Pevensey, where he at once raised [built] a strongly defended castle. Leaving a force of knights in that, he hastened on to Hastings where he quickly raised another.
>
> William of Jumièges, *Deeds of the Dukes of the Normans*, 1071

Near Hastings, William's army defeated Harold who was killed on the field of battle. William became King William I, but he is better known as William the Conqueror. A few years later, some nuns told the story of the Norman Conquest in an embroidery which we call the Bayeux Tapestry.

William had come to England with two or three hundred barons, the most powerful men in Normandy. The new king and his barons had a fighting force of about 3,000–4,000 knights. This small number of Normans now ruled over about $1\frac{1}{2}$ million English. In the first years after the Conquest, they were in great danger from English rebels. In 1068 William had to lead an army north to deal with two rebels, Edwin and Morcar. The story is told by Orderic Vitalis, a monk who had a Norman father and an English mother:

HESTENGA CEASTRA

2 A section of the Bayeux Tapestry showing Normans building a castle.

1 William of Jumièges wrote about two castles. Which one is shown in the Bayeux Tapestry?

2 What does the tapestry tell you about what William of Jumièges meant by a castle?

3a ... the fortresses called castles by the Normans were something new in the English countryside, and so the English, in spite of their courage and love of fighting, could put up only a weak resistance ...

b The king built a castle at Warwick and gave it into the keeping of Henry, son of Roger Beaumont. After that, Edwin, Morcar and other men sought the king's pardon ... Next he built Nottingham Castle and entrusted it to William Peverel.

c When the men of York heard this they were terrified ... and sent the king hostages and the keys of the city. As he was doubtful of their loyalty he fortified a castle in the city and left trustworthy knights to guard it.

Orderic Vitalis, *A History of the Church*, 1141

3 How does Orderic explain that building castles was important in dealing with the rebels?

4 What sort of men were Henry Beaumont and William Peverel?

5 What did the English in York do when they heard of the castles that the king had already built?

The aerial photograph on page 6 shows the ruins of Old Sarum, near the modern city of Salisbury. It helps to explain what Orderic Vitalis meant when he said that castles were new in the English countryside. Around the edge of the hill there is a ditch and earth wall. They were first made about 2,000 years ago by Iron Age people who had farms in the fields around. If an enemy appeared they could take shelter inside their hill-fort. More than a thousand years later, English kings ordered village people to dig the ditch and build the walls again. Old Sarum became another kind of fort known as a burh. It was a place of shelter if Danish armies appeared.

The Iron Age and Anglo-Saxon forts were for village people to shelter in.

4 An aerial photograph of Old Sarum.

1 Look back at the picture from the Bayeux Tapestry on page 5 to help you to find the ruins of a Norman castle in this picture. Why do you think it was smaller than the Anglo-Saxon fort?

The Norman castles had different uses. A castle was the home for one of the new Norman rulers of England and his headquarters for ruling the countryside round and about. There was room for a band of knights who could ride out to deal with any trouble started by the local people.

Where were the castles built?

Orderic tells us that the king kept some castles, like York, under his own control. He handed over the others, like Warwick and Nottingham, to barons. Most barons had a castle in each part of the country where the king granted them land. They were expected to keep law and order there. In return they could collect rents and taxes from the village and town people.

The king and the barons each gave out some of their land to knights in return for certain services. One service the knights had to do was to spend around forty days a year on castle-guard.

There were hundreds of castles by the time William died in 1089. Many were in the border lands between England and Wales. You can read about them in Chapter 6. In the north of England, barons were given castles to deal with Scottish raiders.

The other castles were scattered over the places where there were the largest numbers of Anglo-Saxon people to rule. You can work out some of the reasons for their position from the map of the south-east, opposite.

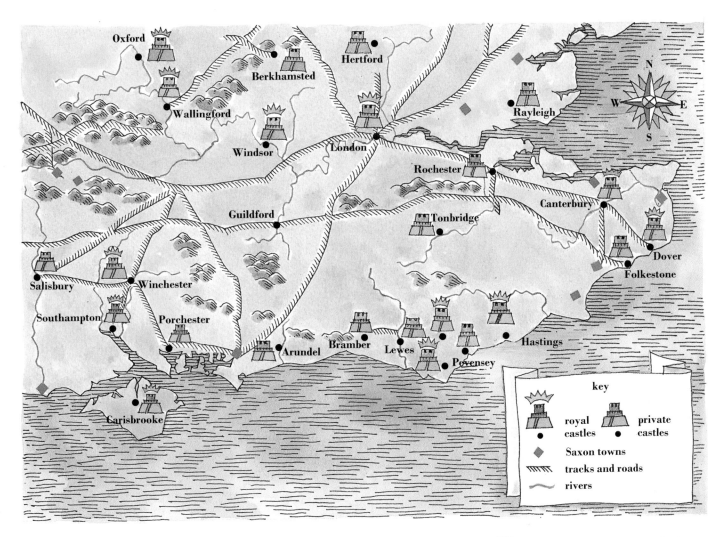

5 The position of Norman castles in south-east England in the first ten years of William the Conqueror's reign.

2 From the map, make lists of castles which guarded these positions (some may appear more than once): river crossings; gaps through hills; crossroads; the coast; Saxon towns.

Building the first Norman castles

William Peveril's castle at Nottingham was built on a steep cliff above the town. That made it quite safe from sudden attack. At Warwick, Henry Beaumont was not so lucky. The land round his castle was flat, even though it was protected on one side by a river. That meant it needed a motte which is the Norman word for a mound. In the hundred years after the Norman Conquest, about a thousand mottes were built in Britain. Today most of them are just grassy hills, but they are one of the best reminders that English, Scots and Welsh people had new rulers after 1066.

A good site for a castle was a place where there had been a fort before, such as at Old Sarum. Along the coast there were remains of stone forts built by the Romans to guard the shores against invaders. These made a good outer defence, but at Cardiff a motte was needed inside the walls to make a stronghold which could be defended by a few knights.

The Bayeux Tapestry shows that Norman soldiers built their own castle

6 Cardiff Castle. The Roman walls are under the present walls which have been rebuilt since then.

1 The local people of Nottingham and Warwick spoke Anglo-Saxon and those at Cardiff spoke Welsh. They could say what they felt about the castles without getting into trouble with the Normans! What sorts of things might they have said about the castles?

2 Look at the reconstruction of a motte and bailey castle opposite.

a Describe the difference between a reconstruction picture and one drawn from imagination.

b Which do you think is most helpful to understanding castles, looking at a reconstruction picture or visiting the ruins? Explain your choice.

at Hastings. But after 1066 the conquered people did the work. The Normans gave them orders to come with digging tools, baskets for shifting soil, axes to cut down trees and carts to carry timber to the building site.

In a town the first job was often to knock down houses to make a clear space. Then hundreds of men (and probably women) carried baskets of earth to the ever-growing mound. When it was high enough, they put up a wooden building for the castle commander who was known as a constable. The king or baron would stay there if he visited.

The motte was usually in one corner of a bailey which was the Norman word for courtyard. There would be many wooden buildings in the bailey. Some were storerooms, kitchens and workshops for the men who made arrows or repaired armour. Some were for the knights on castle-guard and their war-horses, as well as the archers who kept watch day and night. There was a room where the baron could hold a law court and where his officials collected the rents and taxes.

7 A reconstruction picture of a motte and bailey.

3a Which is the motte and which is the bailey?

b What do these words mean?

4 Suppose you were leader of a band of twenty Saxon resistance fighters. Would you risk making an attack on a motte and bailey castle? Explain why or why not.

8 The White Tower today. In Norman times it had a coat of white paint which gave it its name. Its windows were enlarged in the seventeenth century.

The first stone castles

Before about 1100, nearly all castles had wooden buildings and fences. There were just three or four with a stone tower or keep. The best example is the White Tower in London which was built for William I.

William's tower is really a royal palace with the main rooms on top of each other. The way it was built and decorated put across the power and importance of the king. It was the largest and grandest living place in England and it was also the headquarters of the king's government. He could call barons and bishops to meetings in the great hall. There were rooms for them to sleep when they came to attend the king and a chapel for bishops to hold services. In some rooms screens were put up and behind them clerks wrote out the king's letters and charters.

The king had another splendid stone castle at Colchester and the Earl of Hereford built one at Chepstow on the frontiers between Wales and England. These three are the only stone castle buildings from before 1100 which we can still see today.

5 What does the picture tell you about: a) the Tower's defences and b) its other uses?

The Normans and the Church

Bishops and cathedrals

The aerial photograph of Old Sarum shows that the castle was a motte and bailey. The local people, would not have thought that such a roughly-made building was beautiful. What would they have thought about the building that was built where the cross-shaped church ruins can be seen?

The church at Old Sarum was a cathedral. To be a cathedral, a church needs one special item of furniture, a bishop's throne which is a *cathedra* in Latin. Ever since the early days of Christianity there have been bishops who are in charge of all the priests in one part of the country which is called a diocese.

In Anglo-Saxon times, before the Normans came, there were only nine bishops and nine cathedrals in England. William the Conqueror increased the number to seventeen. All but one of the bishops were from Normandy. Work started on new cathedrals. When they were finished many years later, each Norman cathedral was big enough to fit several Anglo-Saxon cathedrals inside. Some Anglo-Saxon cathedrals had been in small, unimportant villages. All the new Norman cathedrals were in towns, with a castle not far away.

The new cathedrals were a sign that bishops were as important as the greatest barons. They took charge of part of the work of the king's government, such as making laws, keeping accounts and being judges. When the king called the most powerful Normans to a meeting of the Great Council,

1 What sort of evidence might Alan Sorrel have used to reconstruct the ruined church at Old Sarum (below)?

9 A reconstruction of the now ruined church at Old Sarum as it would probably have looked in the 1120s. The picture is by Alan Sorrel who drew many reconstructions of old buildings which he tried to make as accurate as possible.

the bishops often had the biggest say in what was decided.

Some bishops were also military leaders. The Bishop of Durham had to keep a force of knights and soldiers to deal with Scottish raiders. The main home of a bishop is called a palace and the Bishop of Durham's palace was a massive castle next to his cathedral. Bishop Roger of Salisbury was not a soldier, but he lived just like a baron. His palace was in the castle at Old Sarum and he also had two more castles built in England and one in Wales.

Priests and monks

In William the Conqueror's time, the men who served God in nine of the cathedrals were monks. Their cathedrals stood in the grounds of a monastery, as you can see in the plan of Durham. The other cathedrals are known as secular cathedrals. Secular means 'living in the outside world', so it tells us that the priests did not live inside monastery walls.

England was the only country with a large number of monastery-cathedrals. This was because of William I's respect for the monks in Normandy. As well as worshipping God, they served Him by helping the poor and running hospitals, schools for boys and colleges for young men. Norman monasteries had large libraries and writing-rooms where monks copied books by hand.

William chose Lanfranc, who was the abbot of the monastery at Caen in Normandy, to be Archbishop of Canterbury. From Lanfranc's time the Archbishop of Canterbury has always been the primate, or head, of all the bishops in England. William and Lanfranc decided which cathedrals should be served by monks. They also increased the number of other monasteries.

William gave land for new monasteries. One of these was Battle Abbey, near Hastings, which was the king's way of giving thanks to God for his victory over Harold. Barons followed the king's example. When they built a castle they often set up a monastery nearby. They believed that gifts for the service of God would help their souls to go to heaven.

William de Warenne was a powerful baron in the south of England. With his wife he visited one of the most famous monasteries in France:

> **11** We found the holiness, piety and devotion there very great . . . It had long been our wish and intention, as advised by Archbishop Lanfranc, to found some religious house for our sins and the safety of our souls . . . So we sent and asked Hugh the abbot and all his holy congregation that they would let us have two, or three, or four monks out of their holy flock and we would give them a church which we had built of stone in place of a wooden church under the castle of Lewes. And we would give it with, at the first, as much land and beasts and goods as would keep twelve monks there . . .

Lewes cartulary [book of charters]

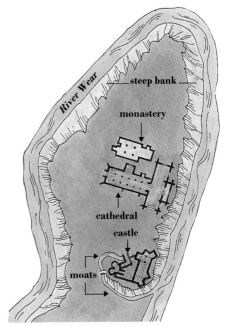

10 The castle and cathedral at Durham.

2 Why did the Normans decide to build the castle and cathedral at Durham in these positions?

3 What sort of 'religious house' did William de Warenne set up at Lewes?

4a Who was Archbishop Lanfranc?

b Why would he be in favour of what William de Warenne did at Lewes?

5a Explain why barons like William gave valuable land to monasteries.

b What do you think was the most important reason?

Abbots and priors

William de Warenne tells us that he asked Hugh the abbot to send him monks. An abbot was head of a monastery known as an abbey. Most important abbeys did the same as Hugh's and set up branch monasteries in other places. The abbot was head of them all, but each one had a prior or 'first monk' in charge. Some were for nuns and the person in charge was a prioress. These branch monasteries were known as priories. The monastery that William de Warenne set up was Lewes Priory.

Some of the most important abbeys were very wealthy, so they could afford churches which were as splendid as cathedrals. After the middle ages some of them did become cathedrals.

The great rebuilding

William of Malmesbury Abbey was a monk who wrote books about the history of the Church and the Norman kings. In one he wrote:

> 12 After their coming to England, they gave new life to the rule of religion which had there grown lifeless. You might see great churches rise in every village, and, in the towns and cities, monasteries built after a style never known before.

William of Malmesbury, *History of Recent Times*, 1142

William wrote seventy-six years after the Norman conquest. By that time the Normans had built or rebuilt all but five of the cathedrals and abbey churches on the map opposite. They were all in a new style copied from Normandy. Lanfranc took the lead. To build his new cathedral in Canterbury he sent for the man who had planned his abbey in Normandy. Other bishops and abbots followed his example. They did not try to save Anglo-Saxon buildings which had often taken centuries to build. If they were in the way they had them knocked down.

1 For each of the five lines in the key, write two sentences to explain what the map opposite tells you about cathedrals and abbey churches in Norman times.

2 Why do you think the Normans did not keep Anglo-Saxon cathedrals and abbey churches?

3 Match up these words with their definitions:

abbot/abbess	A priest who does not live in a monastery
primate	A person in charge of a diocese
prior/prioress	The head of a monastery or group of monasteries
secular	The chief church leader in England and Wales
constable	The head of a monastery set up by an abbey
bishop	The commander of a castle

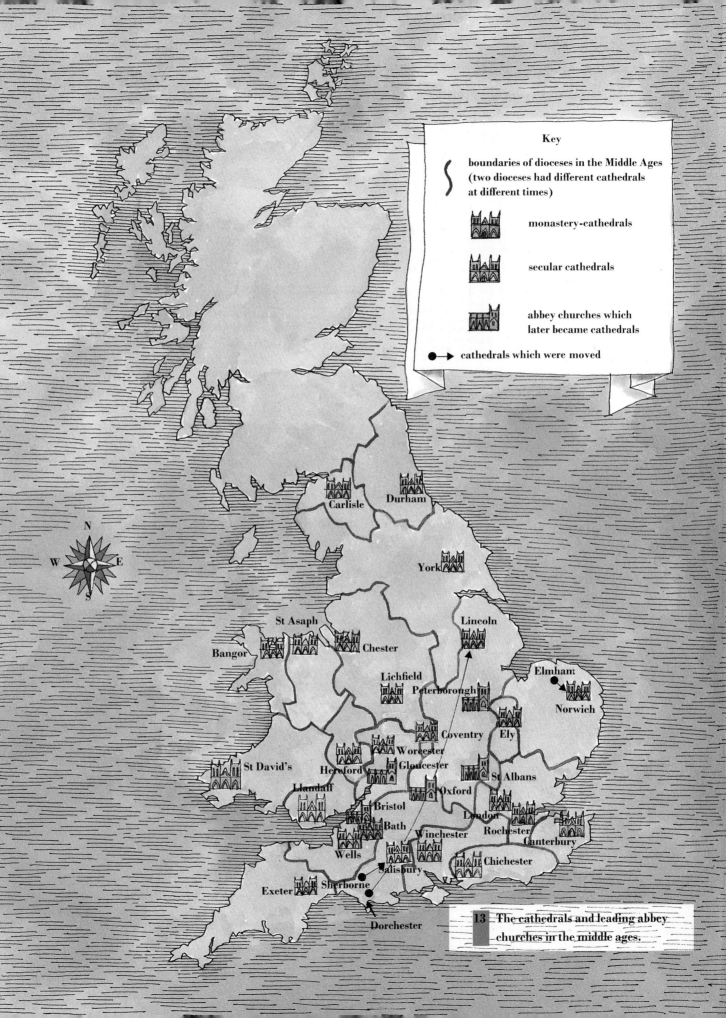

Key

boundaries of dioceses in the Middle Ages
(two dioceses had different cathedrals
at different times)

monastery-cathedrals

secular cathedrals

abbey churches which
later became cathedrals

cathedrals which were moved

Carlisle

Durham

York

St Asaph

Bangor

Chester

Lincoln

Elmham

Norwich

Lichfield

Peterborough

Coventry

Ely

Worcester

St David's

Hereford

Gloucester

St Albans

Llandaff

Oxford

Bristol

London

Bath

Rochester

Winchester

Canterbury

Wells

Chichester

Exeter

Sherborne

Salisbury

Dorchester

13 The cathedrals and leading abbey
churches in the middle ages.

Norman Architecture

1 Make notes and sketches of the shapes which help to identify the style of Norman builders.

2 *Trans* is Latin for 'across'. What is a transept?

3 *Nave* comes from the Latin for 'ship'. Imagine standing on your head in Durham Cathedral and explain why the word is used for the main part of a church.

4 Why are churches built on an east-to-west line?

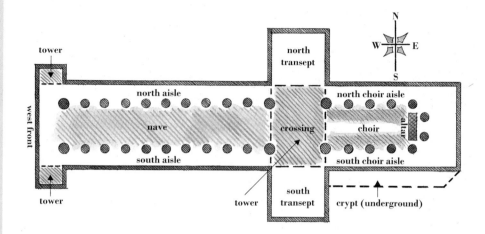

14 Plan of a Norman cathedral.

15 The west door of Lincoln Cathedral.

16 The crypt at Canterbury Cathedral.

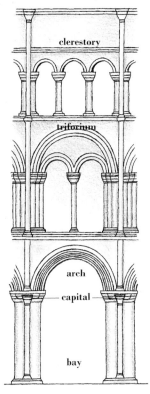

clerestory

triforium

arch

capital

bay

17 Norman arches.

18 Durham Cathedral nave.

Review and Assessment

1 Study this picture of part of Castle Rising.

a What is the name of this part of a castle?

b What building style is it in. Explain how you recognised it.

c From what you have read in this chapter would you expect the stone building at Castle Rising to have been built before or after AD 1100?

2 An Anglo-Saxon born in Durham, Lincoln or Old Sarum in 1050 might (with luck) have lived to around 1100. How might they have explained to a grandchild the changes they had seen since they were teenagers?

3 With the help of the pictures on pages 5–9, say how you would describe some of the differences between a fort and a castle. In which ways are they similar?

4 On page 5 you read that 'the fortresses called castles by the Normans were something new in the English countryside.'

a Explain why this was.

b Would a Norman cathedral or monastery (and the people who served in them) be new in the same way? Explain your answer.

5 In the American west, soldiers, frontiersmen and cowboys took over the land which had been used by Indians for hunting and fishing. How do the castles built by the Normans show that their conquest of the English was different from the conquest of the Indians?

6 The people described in this chapter have been mostly a) barons and knights, or b) bishops and abbots. Explain how each of a) and b) were important to setting up Norman rule in England.

7 William of Malmesbury told the story of Wulfstan, the Bishop of Worcester who was the only Anglo-Saxon bishop in William the Conqueror's kingdom. Wulfstan did the same as other bishops and knocked down the old Saxon cathedral to make way for one in the new Norman style. But he had doubts:

> **20** When the work of building a larger church . . . had gone far enough for the monks to enter into it, orders were given for the old church which the Blessed Oswald [a Saxon bishop] had built, to be unroofed and demolished. Standing beneath the sky while this was being done, Wulfstan could not hold back his tears. For this he was gently rebuked by those who were with him who said that he should be rejoicing that the church was being enriched because a greater number [of monks] needed more spacious buildings. He replied 'I think that we miserable sinners destroy the work of the saints to win ourselves fame . . . We pile up stones neglecting our souls.'
>
> William of Malmesbury, *Deeds of the Kings of the English*, 1125

a Why did the people with Wulfstan think it was right to knock down the old Saxon building?
b Why did Wulfstan have doubts about whether it was the right thing to do?
c 'The new building in Worcester was a real improvement and not just a change in fashion.' What would you say to (i) support this and (ii) disagree with this statement?
d Can you think of a case where it might be better to keep something old rather than replace it with something more splendid?

8 By the 1100s, there were two or three stone castles (like the White Tower) in England and more than twenty new cathedrals or large abbey churches nearly finished.
a Why do you think there were more fine churches than grand castles?
b Would England have been ruled in a better or worse way if it had been the other way about?

2 The castle in war

Rebels and bad neighbours

In William the Conqueror's reign it usually did not matter much whether the king, a baron or a bishop controlled a castle. They were all Normans and they all had to stand together against the English.

Things were different when William II became king in 1087. Some Norman barons and bishops wanted his older brother to be king and they rebelled. The rebels were led by Odo who was the new king's uncle. He was a bishop in Normandy and Earl of Kent in England. The *Anglo-Saxon Chronicle* takes up the story:

> 1　Each of them went to his castle and manned it and stocked it with food and equipment . . . Bishop Odo . . . went to Kent to his earldom . . . laid waste the king's land and the archbishop's and carried all the goods into his castle.
>
> *Anglo-Saxon Chronicle*, 1087

The *Chronicle* was describing a problem which upset the peace for the next 200 years. A baron needed only a small band of knights and a castle to cause trouble. If they had enough stores in the castle it was difficult to get them out. Meanwhile they could make raids into the countryside and lay it waste – which means burning farms and taking food and other goods back into their castle.

The king sent an army after Odo who had led his men into Pevensey Castle. They carried out a siege for six weeks. Siege comes from the French word for seat or sitting – *siège*. At Pevensey the king's army probably did just that. They camped outside the castle to stop anyone bringing food in. After six weeks the defenders' food ran out and Odo surrendered. The king took away his earldom and made him leave England.

In 1095 the Earl of Northumbria rebelled and sheltered in his castle built on a high rock at Bamburgh on the sea coast. The king arrived with his army and the *Anglo-Saxon Chronicle* tells us what he decided to do:

> **2** ... when the king saw he could not take it by force of arms, he ordered a castle to be built in front of Bamburgh, and in his language called it 'Malveisin', that is in English 'Bad Neighbour', and garrisoned it [filled it with soldiers] strongly with his men.
>
> *Anglo-Saxon Chronicle*, 1095

The modern French for 'bad neighbour' is *mal voisin*. The king's castle was a bad neighbour because his men could climb to its top to fire their arrows over the fences of Bamburgh. It was probably not a true castle but a wooden tower.

How castles were made stronger

In 1100 William II died and his brother became King Henry I. One of the big problems he faced was that barons were making their castles stronger. Usually they built stone walls and a stone gatehouse. An important reason for this was that an easy way of breaking into a castle was to set fire to its wooden defences. The new gatehouse also made a more comfortable home for the constable or the baron than the wooden building on the motte.

Henry did not allow barons to build private castles in stone unless he gave them a licence. He gave one to the Earl of Oxford who built a stone keep for his castle at Hedingham. The Earl of Cornwall had a licence and decided to build a stone wall round the top of his motte at Trematon castle. Henry I, himself, had stone defences added to his own castles, such as the one at Corfe.

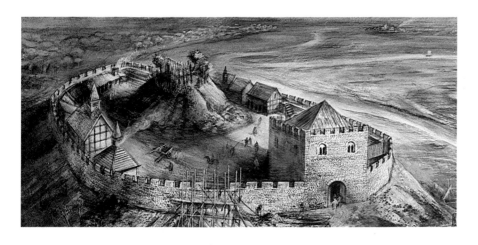

1 What sort of castle would the king have ordered to be built (source 2)?
2 This section has described two ways of forcing a castle to surrender. What were they?

3 Compare this with the picture of a motte and bailey on page 9. How was it a) easier to defend, and b) more comfortable to live in?
4 Why should the king be worried about stone castles?

3 How a baron strengthened his private castle at Bramber (see map, page 7).

Stone castles of the early twelfth century

4 The stone keep at Hedingham.

spiral staircase in this tower

dormitory floor
– beds for the lord and his wife,
and straw on the floor for everyone else

great hall
– home for the lord and his guests.
It was two storeys high

garrison lived here
kitchens
armourers workshop
stores

the only way in is up the stairway.
This was covered with a building
to stop attack from rushing
at the entrance

31m

24m

0m

---

5 The stone wall at Trematon would have looked like this one at Restormel. Walls like these are called shell keeps.

1 Why was a shell keep a good way of strengthening a motte and bailey castle?

2 Explain how crenellation would have been used.

6 Defences of a curtain wall.

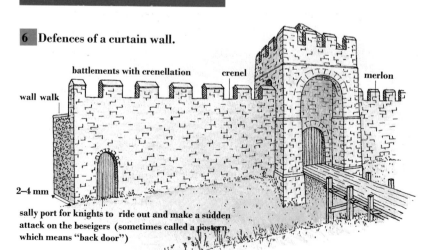

battlements with crenellation   crenel   merlon

wall walk

2–4 mm

sally port for knights to ride out and make a sudden
attack on the beseigers (sometimes called a postern
which means "back door")

How to capture a castle

In 1120 Henry I's sons were drowned when the White Ship sank in the English Channel. When the king died in 1132 it was his cousin, Stephen, who became king and many barons rebelled against him. Henry's rules against castle building were ignored. The *Anglo-Saxon Chronicle* explained it like this:

> **7** Every man built castles and held the country against him and they filled the country full of castles . . .
>
> . . . that lasted the nineteen years while Stephen was king.
>
> *Anglo-Saxon Chronicle*, 1137

Hundreds of unlicensed castles were built. A rebel baron could use his castle as a strong base to collect food and stores from the countryside around. He could keep his law courts going and collect the fees and fines from them. In these places the king's sheriffs (officials in charge of counties) could not collect money and taxes for Stephen or see that the royal law courts were run properly and fairly.

The only sure way for Stephen to deal with a rebel was to capture his castle. By this time there were different kinds of siege engines to help an attack. Stephen used some of them when he besieged Exeter castle. A chronicler tells us what happened:

> **8** Exeter is a large city, ranking they say, the fourth in England . . . Its castle stands on a lofty mound protected by uncapturable walls, and towers of hewn stone . . .
>
> . . . the garrison, manning the battlements and towers with glittering arms, taunted the king and his followers as they approached the walls. Sometimes they made unexpected sallies and fell furiously on the royal army; at others they shot arrows and launched missiles against them from above . . .
>
> Meanwhile the king . . . raised lofty wooden towers, from which the defenders of the castle were attacked. Day and night he persevered [kept on] with the siege . . . causing his slingers to annoy them by hurling stones. He also employed miners to sap the fortifications and had all manner of machines constructed, some of great height to overlook what was passing [going on] within the garrison, and others on a level with the foundation of the walls which they intended to batter down.
>
> *Deeds of King Stephen*, 1147–53

3 Look at the pictures on page 20. List all the problems there would be for enemies trying to capture a) a rectangular keep like Hedingham, and b) a shell keep like the one at Restormel.

4 Look at source 8. Why would Exeter castle be difficult to capture?

5 Which exits would the garrison use to make a sally?

6 The word sap comes from the Latin *sappa* which means a pick or pickaxe. What does to 'sap the fortifications' mean?

7 List the three other kinds of attack that the king's army used.

Siege weapons

9 In Stephen's time.

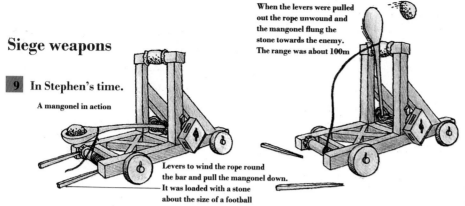

A mangonel in action

When the levers were pulled out the rope unwound and the mangonel flung the stone towards the enemy. The range was about 100m

Levers to wind the rope round the bar and pull the mangonel down.

It was loaded with a stone about the size of a football

A battering ram

animal hides

ditch filled with stones, logs, earth, straw etc.

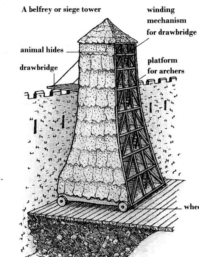

A belfrey or siege tower

winding mechanism for drawbridge

animal hides

drawbridge

platform for archers

wheels

moat filled in

10 Fifty years later.

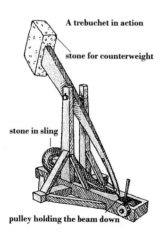

A trebuchet in action

stone for counterweight

stone in sling

pulley holding the beam down

A trebuchet was more powerful than a mangonel. It was also more reliable because the mangonel rope could tangle or go soft in the rain. Trebuchet operators were skilled men who could calculate how far a stone would go and could hit the same part of a wall with most of their shots to weaken it. Stones

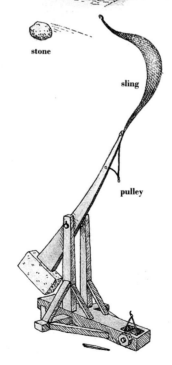

stone

sling

pulley

hitting the inner walls were deadly because they would shatter into fragments and act like a grenade.

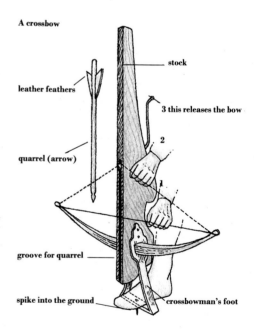

A crossbow

stock

leather feathers

3 this releases the bow

quarrel (arrow)

2

groove for quarrel

spike into the ground

crossbowman's foot

Crossbows were not new but they became much more deadly around the 1180s when the stock was given a new design.

Mining

In 1216 a civil war broke out. On one side were King John and many of the barons and bishops who believed he should remain king. On the other side were other barons and bishops who claimed that John had broken the promises he made when he had signed Magna Carta in 1215.

In most parts of England the constables in royal castles stayed loyal to John but his enemies still held some important castles. One was Rochester which guarded a main road into London, so John decided that it must be captured. He knew that it would not be easy because the castle had a strong stone keep, like the one at Hedingham (page 20), and a stone curtain wall. There was a large garrison of a hundred knights and many archers and crossbowmen.

Soon quarrels and stones were humming through the air in both directions over the castle walls. John's army used five siege engines and his archers worked in shifts. The defenders were often forced to flee from the battlements but the royal army could not get through the curtain wall. So the king called for miners.

Miners were skilled men. In peace time they tunnelled into hill-sides for lead, copper or tin. At Rochester they started a tunnel a safe distance away from the castle and dug through the earth towards the curtain wall. When they were underneath they dug out a large space and held up its roof with wooden props. Then they filled the space with firewood and set it alight. The fire burned the wooden props, the roof fell in and the wall above collapsed.

John's men could now rush into the bailey, but the strong rebel force simply retreated into the keep which had its own well and food supplies. So the miners were told to dig under one of the corner towers. They got there on 25 November and started to dig out a huge underground chamber. John sent an urgent message to London:

> 11 We command you that with all haste by day and night, you send to us 40 bacon pigs of the fattest and those less good for eating to bring fire under the tower.
>
> King John, 1216

When the pigs were cooked, the fat ran out and cooled into chunks of lard. On 30 November the miners packed these round the wooden props under the corner of the keep and set them alight. An hour or two later the tower cracked and began to slide into the space below. The defenders came out and surrendered. Today, if you visit Rochester castle you will find it has three square towers and a round one in the corner the miners destroyed.

5 Can you suggest any ways of defending a castle against miners?

How to defend a castle

After Stephen died, Henry II (1154–89) and John (1200–16) spent huge sums of money on stronger defences for royal castles. They were needed now that the trebuchet had been invented and attackers had learned how to use squads of crossbowmen to fire quarrels so that they fell down like rain on the enemy.

12 Dover: Henry and John's most powerful castle

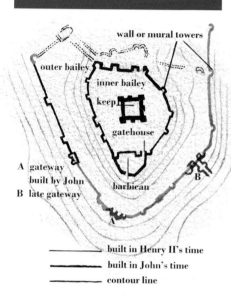

wall or mural towers

outer bailey

inner bailey

keep

gatehouse

A gateway built by John

B late gateway

barbican

———— built in Henry II's time

———— built in John's time

———— contour line

Keeping the enemy away

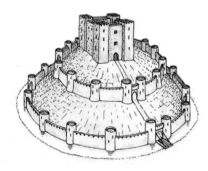

Dover was the first concentric castle. That means its defences were in rings with the same centre. Archers could fire over the next one or two walls at an approaching enemy

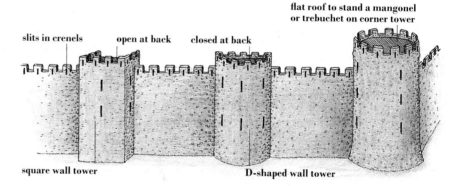

flat roof to stand a mangonel or trebuchet on corner tower

slits in crenels   open at back   closed at back

square wall tower   D-shaped wall tower

Castle often had only a small guard. Once attackers got close to the walls with ladders or ropes with hooks on the end they might get in and outnumber the defenders. So it was important to have curtain walls with places where a few archers could deal with attackers coming in different directions.

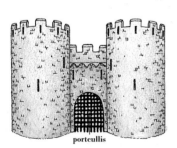

portcullis

If the enemy got close

Single gatehouses were replaced by two towers guarding the entrance. A portcullis could now be used.

A splay at the base of a tower or keep made it harder to sap. If defenders dropped stones they would shatter aand send pieces among the enemy.

A barbican was a small extra bailey in front of the gatehouse. It forced the enemy to pack close together.

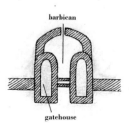

barbican

gatehouse

After the siege of Rochester one man said that 'people no longer put their trust in castles'. Even Dover had been nearly captured when miners got under the gateway (see A on the plan) in 1217. The castle was only just saved and a new gatehouse was made by fitting five D-shaped towers together (B on the plan).

Many lords decided to treat their castle as just a home and not a place for defence. But the king and a few wealthy lords added to the defences of their castles so they were almost impossible to capture. One was Kenilworth.

In 1266 Kenilworth was the centre of one of the longest sieges ever. It began after King Henry III had defeated a rebel, Simon de Montfort. Simon's son shut himself up in Kenilworth with many knights and men-at-arms.

When the king started the siege, the ground in front of the castle must have looked like a building site. Carpenters were making siege engines, towers and battering rams. Men were at work splitting stones into the right size and weight. Gangs of labourers were digging level places to stand the siege engines on. Carts rumbled in with arrows and crossbows by the thousand.

In the end the king's army decided that it would cost less in wages and equipment to sit and wait until the defenders were starving. It took six months.

The plan above shows the defences at Kenilworth. When you look at the strongest and largest castles you can usually see examples of these defences built in the thirteenth and fourteenth centuries.

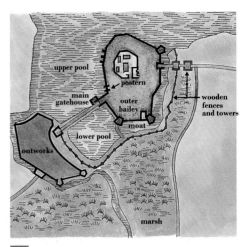

13 Kenilworth in 1266.

water – impossible to mine

outworks with mounds and ditches – difficult to use siege engines

strong curtain walls with towers

very large corner towers

strong gateways

a narrow approach to the gateway

14 Warwick Castle's new corner towers. Look carefully at the top. The jutting out parts are called machicolation. What do you think they were used for?

15 How machicolation developed.

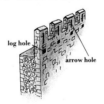

A In the thirteenth century battlements often had arrow slits and a log hole.

B The log hole was used to support a hoarding which jutted out from the wall. Defenders could fire arrows down at attackers or drop rocks, boiling oil, or water.

C In the fourteenth century, hoardings were often replaced with stonework which had holes for firing downwards. These holes are called machicolation. You can also find machicolation in the roofs of gateway passages.

Review and Assessment

1 Look at these pictures:

Motte and bailey (page 9)   Hedingham Castle (page 20)

Bramber Castle (page 19)   Dover Castle (page 24)

Make a chart like this (using a full page) and fill it in:

	Points of defence	Main living spaces
Motte and Bailey Bramber Hedingham Dover		

2 Give two reasons why motte and bailey castles were changed into castles like Bramber.

3 Many stone keeps like Hedingham were built in the reigns of Henry I and Stephen. The baron who paid for one would have given different reasons for building it to a) the castle constable, b) his wife, and c) the king. Write down or set out the reasons he might have given to each of the three.

4 Look at the picture and plan of Dover (page 24). Here are some possible causes of the way it was changed in the reigns of Henry and John:

new understanding of how to strengthen walls and buildings

new siege weapons

the growth of royal power and wealth

John's quarrels with the barons

a Explain how each of these causes played a part in the changes.

b Describe how the strength of castles such as Dover led to changes in the number of castles and the way they were built.

5 Discuss which of the causes of the changes at Dover was the most important. Give reasons for your choice.

6 In 1066 knights were the most important part of an army. By the 1200s people such as crossbowmen, miners and siege-engine makers were just as important. Give examples to show how this change was connected with the changes in castle building and in methods of attack.

3 The castle in peace

Households on the move

1 A baggage cart.

1 Can you think of reasons why local people would be a) pleased, and b) dismayed to see this party arriving?

This was a common sight in the middle ages. The king and the leading barons had castles in different parts of the country. They were always on the move, staying at their different homes for a few days at a time. Two groups of people travelled with them. These were the **retinue** (following) of knights and squires and the **household** of staff and servants.

The kings and barons moved about mainly because it was the only way to stay in control of their kingdom and their lands. They needed to show off their power, collect taxes and rents, hold courts to issue orders and trials to punish wrong-doers.

Near each castle were manors which the king or baron owned. The people who lived there had to supply food for the castle when its owner and his household moved in. Seventy people and a dozen carts needed about a hundred

1 What did the clerk mean by 'by the king's writ' in source 2?

horses. In a few days the people and horses would eat all the food the local manors could supply.

One of Henry II's clerks wrote saying how much the king would pay for food when he stayed at Salisbury Castle (a measure would have been about enough to fill half a modern bath):

> **2** ... in the stocking of Salisbury Castle for 125 measures of corn £21 by the king's writ. And for 120 bacons £10 6 8d. Also for 400 cheeses £8. And for 20 measures of beans 60s. And for 20 measures of salt by the same writ.

Other orders went out for manors to send in cattle, pigs and sheep, hens and ducks, eggs by the hundred and huge amounts of hay and oats for the horses. Village people were told to get ready to work as servants, kitchenhands, stablemen, blacksmiths, cart menders and so on. If the orders came in winter they would be glad of the extra pence they would earn. If they had to work in the castle in the summer, their crops and harvest could suffer.

After a few days the king or baron would move on. Often they left behind just the constable and a small guard, but sometimes the baron's wife stayed longer in one castle with her own smaller household.

3 The great hall at Hedingham Castle.

Living in a castle

It was hard to fit so many people into a castle where the only main building was a square keep. Look at the plan of Hedingham (page 20). Like all keeps it had one large room, the **great hall**.

The retinue and household all lived here. They ate at trestle tables which were cleared away afterwards because the hall was the only place to spend time when the weather was bad. It was sometimes used as a courtroom. There were screens in one corner to cut off the clerks writing letters and doing accounts. In some castles a removeable altar was set up for morning mass. At night the retinue and the most important people in the household slept there on mattresses or lying on the rushes on the floor.

Only the baron and his wife had their own rooms, on the floor above the hall. One was the **bedchamber**. The bed was often their most valuable possession and it travelled with them. Curtains were hung round at night so the sleepers could not be seen by servants.

The **solar** was the sitting room used mostly by the baron's wife and the females of her household. The **wardrobe** was the room where the family clothes and an iron-bound box for storing money, jewels and gold or silver. The baron had a small chapel where his family could hear mass in private.

The **garderobe** was a small space in the wardrobe wall. It was the privy or toilet and it emptied into the moat if there was one. If not, it went into a cesspool. When Henry III was moving to the Tower of London he ordered:

> **4** Since the privy in the chamber of our wardrobe in London is situated in an unsuitable place, wherefore it smells badly, we command you in no way to neglect seeing that another privy chamber is made.

From the thirteenth century onwards, castles began to be less crowded. If the outer defences were made stronger with gatehouses, barbicans and wall-towers, the inside could be made more comfortable.

Chepstow (source 5) was a castle in the new style. In its early days it had a single stone keep. By 1300 it had a new great hall with large windows. There were separate buildings for the baron and the top men in the household as well as lodgings for guests and their servants.

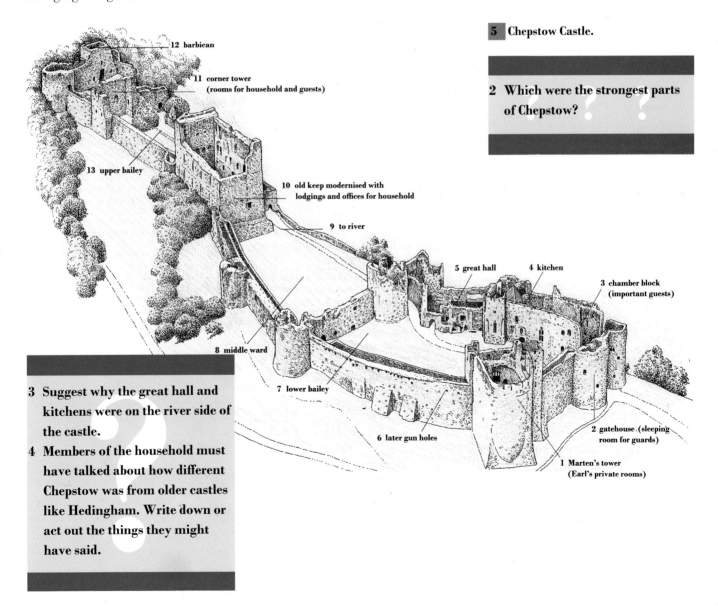

12 barbican
11 corner tower (rooms for household and guests)
13 upper bailey
10 old keep modernised with lodgings and offices for household
9 to river
8 middle ward
7 lower bailey
6 later gun holes
5 great hall
4 kitchen
3 chamber block (important guests)
2 gatehouse (sleeping room for guards)
1 Marten's tower (Earl's private rooms)

5 Chepstow Castle.

2 Which were the strongest parts of Chepstow?

3 Suggest why the great hall and kitchens were on the river side of the castle.

4 Members of the household must have talked about how different Chepstow was from older castles like Hedingham. Write down or act out the things they might have said.

The household at work

The day began at sunrise. The first duty was to hear a priest say mass. To be at mass you must have gone without food – or fasted. After mass you could 'break fast' with a snack of bread washed down with ale or watered wine. It would be still early when work started.

The seneschal or steward of the lands was in charge of all the manors, market places and courts where the baron was lord. He had to see that the reeves in charge of them did their job well and collected all the rents, market fees and court fines. In a day's work the seneschal might hold a court in the great hall. After that he could see a reeve who had come to report. The rest of the time he would need for dictating letters which were written down by clerks.

The wardrober or treasurer took the money which came into the household, paid the bills and kept careful accounts. He got the name 'wardrober' from Norman times when he was in charge of the box in the wardrobe. An important baron's wardrober would have his own office with clerks who counted money on a chequer board which they used like an abacus.

The chaplain had several duties. He was in charge of the chapels and the priests. He gave orders to the almoner who handed out left-over food and cast-off clothes to the poor. The almoner's name comes from alms, the word used for help given to the poor. Most important, the chaplain looked after the clerks who wrote out the household letters and accounts.

The steward of the house took charge of all the indoor servants – cooks, table-servers, doorkeepers and the laundress. Each day he kept a careful record of the food, drink, candle wax and so on that he had bought.

The marshal supervised the outdoor servants. There were grooms and blacksmiths for the horses, kennel men and falconers for the hunting dogs and birds, cart makers and drivers getting ready for the next move, and armourers and fletchers (arrow makers). Often the marshal had to arrange a morning's sport. This might be a deer hunt. At other times there would be hawking which the ladies often joined in.

Dinner

The main meal came five hours after sunrise, when the day's work or hunting was done. Barons' families in the great hall with their guests at the top table. The rest of the retinue and household sat at tables down the length of the hall.

Bread was eaten with every course. Day-old bread was used as plates for the meat and fish. When the countess gave dinner in Kenilworth castle just to her own household and two guests in 1245, the steward had to arrange for $1\frac{1}{2}$ oxen, 3 sheep, 2 kids, about 300 eggs and several hens.

After dinner there might be entertainers. Minstrels, dancers, jugglers and acrobats were all very popular. The day came to an end when the sun set.

1 **Explain:**
  a **the difference between a wardrobe and garderobe.**
  b **where the word 'breakfast' comes from.**
  c **why the seneschal was thought of as the head of the household.**
  d **the three main duties of the chaplain's department and why the chaplain was the most suitable person to be in charge of them.**
2 **Look at the picture. What do you notice about a) the table, and b) how the people ate?**

6 Dinner in the great hall.

How to become a lady or a knight

Girls in noble families were often betrothed (promised to a future husband) as infants. Most were married at fourteen or not long after. Before that they were sent to be taught by nuns to be a lady-in-waiting, or damsel, to be a baron's wife. She would see that the girl was taught reading and writing, but expected her to spend more time learning singing, dancing and embroidery.

Barons and knights often placed their sons in another lord's household. Young boys began as pages who served one or two knights. Their hard day began by helping their masters to dress. After breakfast there would be lessons in reading, writing and Latin from one of the chaplain's priests. That could be followed by lessons in singing and dancing and training for a knight's outdoor life. They might practice fighting with light wooden swords or be sent out to hold the dogs on a hawking trip.

An older boy became a knight's squire. He would learn to ride the massive war-horses and to use an adult-sized sword and a lance.

The tournament

The plan of Kenilworth Castle on page 25 shows a causeway, or raised road, between the upper and lower pool. It was an easily guarded way into the castle but it was also used as the tiltyard. Other castles had their tiltyards in a level space outside the curtain walls.

Tiltyards were for knights to practise fighting. This was important for them and for their horses which had to become used to the excitement of battle and the jolts caused when knights clashed with their lances at twenty miles an hour. There were few other chances to train war-horses. They cost about two years' pay, so the knight never used them for hunting. When the retinue moved between castles, the knight rode a smaller horse called a palfrey.

In Norman castles, knights held a mock battle known as a *melée*, the French word for 'free for all'. Two teams charged at each other, riding knee to knee. Their lances and swords were blunted but the idea was to force the other team's knights off their horses and then to fight on the ground.

Later, melées were turned into public shows or tournaments. Stands were put up for the women of the household, guests and people from the town. Knights travelled around the country to take part. But these tournaments were like some football matches today. Tempers rose and knights fought on after they were ordered to finish. Their squires often joined in.

In the fourteenth century, kings and barons cleaned up the tournaments. *Melées* were stopped and the tournaments were turned into a day's programme of jousts between two knights. In the first round they charged at each other down each side of a wooden barrier. If both were still seated after the charge they turned and rode at each other again. Afterwards they fought a second round on foot until one fell to his knees or lost his sword.

7 A lady playing a dulcimer which was an early version of the piano.

8 Tournaments were important social events. The king and queen watch the Earl of Warwick tilting at another baron. The barons' pages ride alongside.

3 Why are the umpires on the left checking lances in source 8?

4 Look at the Earl's helmet and his page's coat. Can you see a link?

Heraldry

The badge of the earls of Warwick was a bear and ragged staff. Such badges went back to the Normans who nailed them on to their shields. They were needed because one knight dressed in armour from head to toe looked just like any other knight.

Barons and knights chose simple designs such as a coloured stripe or the picture of a flower, animal or bird. When King Henry I chose a lion it was meant to be a symbol of royal strength. Others were made up from the names of families. The knights of the Trumpington family wore two trumpets.

As families joined together by marriage they combined parts of each other's shields. King Edward III divided his into four quarters. He put his lions into two and the French *fleur de lys* into the others as a sign that he claimed to be king of France.

These badges were very important at tournaments. Before a joust a knight wore a loose top-coat decorated with his 'arms' which is why we talk of a coat of arms. He dressed his page and his horse in the same arms and put them on a banner outside his changing tent. The person in charge of the ceremonies was the herald. He announced the names for each joust and took pride in being able to identify them from their coats of arms.

In 1484 the king set up the College of Heralds to lay down strict rules about who could have arms and what should be on them. Not long after this, tournaments came to an end. They had no use now the age of cannon and muskets had arrived, which made the knights' skills useless. Noble families still kept their coats of arms but the College of Heralds was more busy with new ones for towns, universities and business companies. It is still at work and describes coats of arms in words which have come down from the middle ages.

1 Not all lords' sons became squires. Some were sent to schools run by cathedrals and abbeys. From there they might become a priest, possibly even a bishop, or they might become officials in the king's government or judges in his law courts. Suppose you lived at the time: which would you have preferred, the life of a knight, or being an official or judge?

2 Young women were not given the chance to train for any work which took them outside the castle. Why do you think this was?

9 Matthew Paris used shields to decorate a book he wrote in the 1250s. These (left) are upside down because he is writing about men who were killed in the crusades.

10 You can often see coats of arms on brass plates in churches but the colours have worn away. This (right) shows one of the Trumpington knights.

Review and Assessment

1 Study this reconstruction of dinner in the great hall in Conwy Castle built in the 1280s.

   a Was it in a keep or a separate building like Chepstow's (page 29)? What evidence have you used for your answer?

   b Which are the most important people? How do you know?

   c Find a page and the steward of the household. How does the picture help to explain what their jobs were?

   d Would the people in the room feel safe from attack? Explain why.

2 Look at sources 6, 7 and 8. What do they tell you about the differences between men and women in a baron's family?

3 The painting above is a reconstruction by a modern artist. Look at the picture from the middle ages on page 30.

   a Do you think the modern artist might have studied it before he made his painting? Explain how you have decided.

    b Suppose there is only space for either the painting from the time or the reconstruction. You have to choose one to explain what dinner in the great hall was like.

       i)   Give reasons for choosing the reconstruction.

      ii) Give reasons for choosing the painting of the time.

     iii) Say which you have chosen and why.

---

4   Use the picture of Dover Castle to plan a visit for the class with five stops to study the defences. Make notes (with sketches where they are helpful) of what the class should look for at these five stops.

---

5   You have to choose one picture for the cover of a folder of work on castles 1066–1500. Your choice has to be made from these pictures:

A Building a castle at Hastings – page 5

B The White Tower – page 9

C Reconstruction of a motte and bailey – page 9

D Dover Castle – page 24

E Warwick Castle – page 25

F A household on the move – page 27

G A tournament – page 31

None of them gives a complete picture of the history of castles so you must choose the one which comes closest to explaining what castles were and how they were important. Obviously, you should not choose one which misleads readers about what they will find in the folder.

    a For each picture make a brief note under these headings:

       i)   How it illustrates an important part of the castle story.

      ii) How it might mislead readers about the history of castles.

    b Number the pictures 1–7 in the order of your choice.

---

6   Pictures A to G show two different kinds of illustration. A F and G are pictures made in the middle ages. B C D and E come from books which would be read by tourists today. Give examples of ways each *kind* of illustration can miss out information helpful to understanding everyday castle life.

4 To the glory of God

1 Lincoln Cathedral nave.

The nave: the townspeople's cathedral

Look at the picture of the nave at Lincoln Cathedral (left). Imagine standing here 650 years ago in the 1240s. There are no electric lights and no pulpit. You may be from Lincoln town or a pilgrim who has walked fifty miles. Light streams through the windows and reflects from the shining marble floor. The sound of singing echoes from the roof and the scent of the burning herbs used to make sweet-smelling incense drifts towards you.

You are looking towards the west door. If you looked east your view was blocked by a rood screen across the end of the nave. Rood is the Anglo-Saxon word for cross which tells us that it held a figure of Christ being crucified. The rood screen cut off the nave from the rest of the church, which was reserved for priests and monks.

People did not come into the nave for ordinary Sunday services because they were expected to go to their own parish churches. Yet the nave was always open and townspeople must have come in often. It was the most magnificent public building that most would ever see.

A few times a year there would be religious festivals, especially on Ascension Day (when Christ ascended to heaven) and on the day of the saint the cathedral was dedicated to. Parish priests would lead their congregations to the nave. The cathedral priests would process round in their finest vestments (robes), led by boys carrying crosses and censers – which held incense. A priest under a canopy carried the wafers for mass (see page 38) in a richly decorated vase. They would stop at different places for music and prayers, and finish with a mass at an altar in front of the rood screen.

Beyond the screen: the priests' and monks' cathedral

2 The places of worship inside Lincoln Cathedral.

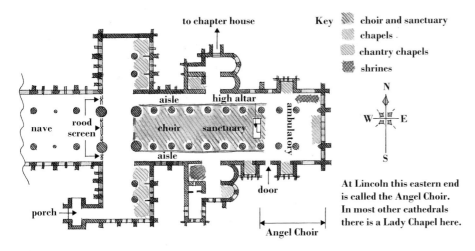

Key — choir and sanctuary / chapels / chantry chapels / shrines

At Lincoln this eastern end is called the Angel Choir. In most other cathedrals there is a Lady Chapel here.

One way of looking at this part of a cathedral is to study it as a beautiful shell covering many places of worship which are each like smaller churches. Priests and monks could go between them in procession, round the aisles and the ambulatory (see the plan above).

The choir

The choir made up one half of the main 'church' within the cathedral. The other half was the sanctuary.

Lincoln was a secular cathedral served by priests. They came into the choir seven times a day to chant psalms and other sacred music, to pray and to hear readings from the Bible. These services were called the 'hours' because they were held at regular times. Because music was so important, people spoke of 'singing the hours'. Monks had an extra service in the middle of the night.

Vigils (Latin for 'keeping watch') — Only monks, at 2.00 or 3.00am
Matins (French for 'morning') — Before dawn
or **Lauds** (Latin for 'praise')
Prime (Latin for 'first') — First hour of the day, about 6.00am
Terce (Latin for 'third') — Third hour of the day, about 9.00am
Sext (Latin for 'sixth') — Midday
Nones (Latin for 'ninth') — Ninth hour of the day, about 3.00pm
Evensong or **vespers** — Late afternoon
Compline (Latin for 'completed') — After sundown

3 The only stone rood screen still standing is in St Albans Cathedral.

1 What does the rood screen do to the view from west to east?

4 A procession on Corpus Christi (Body of Christ) day, about 1400.

2 Most festivals and holiday carnivals in the middle ages included religious processions like this. What does that tell you about people of the time compared with those who take part in present-day carnivals?

5 Monks chanting psalms from a thirteenth-century manuscript (left).
6 Underneath a choir seat in Lincoln Cathedral (right).

5 Monks chanting psalms from a thirteenth-century manuscript (left).
6 Underneath a choir seat in Lincoln Cathedral (right).

1 Stall means standing-place. Where else is the word used?
2 Misericord is from the Latin for 'merciful'. What mercy would a misericord give to an old priest?

Priests and monks stood for many parts of the services. Choir stalls had tip-up seats with ledges underneath. They are known as misericords and were often carved with scenes of everyday life, animals or mythical stories.

The sanctuary

Sanctuary means 'holy place' and it held the high altar which was raised up on some steps. Each day there was a high mass at the altar. Mass commemorated the last supper when Christ gave bread and wine to the disciples saying 'this is my body and blood'.

The priests or monks sang in the choir while another priest celebrated (performed) the mass. He began by calling for blessings on wine and special wafers of bread. He had assistants known as deacons who were younger men who would be priests themselves one day. The most solemn moment came when he raised the bread towards the high altar. He was following Christ's orders to the disciples: 'Do this in remembrance of me'.

7 A priest celebrating mass from a painting of about 1393.

Chapels

A chapel was a separate place of worship with its own sanctuary and altar. The most important chapel was behind the high altar. This was usually the Lady Chapel which was dedicated to Our Lady, the Virgin Mary, mother of Christ. Priests and monks went there for a mass once a week and often every day. Around the east end of the cathedral there were side chapels to other saints.

3 Explain what is happening in the lower and the upper scenes in source 7.
4 Why do you think the painter linked the two?

Chantries and shrines

People in the middle ages believed that each person had a soul. After death the soul could go on to heaven, but that was unlikely unless you had led a really good and saintly life. If you had been a sinner your soul could go straight to the everlasting flames of hell. Most likely it would go to purgatory, a sort of testing place where you suffered for your sins but might, in the end, pass on to heaven.

One way of helping your soul reach heaven was to do a service to God. Barons did this when they gave land to set up monasteries. Another way was to have a daily mass chanted for your soul after death. Rich families arranged for this by a chantry, which was money to pay for a priest to chant the mass.

The best chantry gave enough money to help the church as well. Some left money so that the chantry priest could start a school. Others paid for a chapel in the cathedral. You can see nine of them in the plan of Lincoln.

Most people had no money to leave for chantries. For them the best way of helping their soul was to go on a pilgrimage to pray at a shrine which held the bones of a saint. The main shrine in Lincoln held the head of St Hugh.

8 **The Lady Chapel at Lichfield Cathedral.**

5 Which part is the sanctuary?
6 How does this help to explain that cathedrals were like shells covering many different churches?

The pilgrims

A rhyme you sometimes hear today is 'March winds and April showers bring forth May flowers'. They also bring forth the thought of summer trips into the countryside. Six hundred years ago Geoffrey Chaucer started to write his poem, *The Canterbury Tales*. In modern English it begins:

9
When in April the sweet showers fall . . .
Then people long to go on pilgrimages . . .
And specially from every shire's end
Of England, down to Canterbury they wend . . .

Chaucer, *The Canterbury Tales*, Prologue, 1387

Chaucer's pilgrims went to Canterbury to the shrine which held the body of St Thomas Becket. He was an archbishop who quarrelled with King Henry II. Four knights believed the king wanted him dead. In December 1170 they stabbed Thomas to death while he was at prayer in his cathedral.

Stories of the wonderful power of the dead Archbishop spread fast. A monk wrote this only a few weeks after the murder:

10
. . . the palsied [paralysed people or stroke victims] are cured, the blind see, the deaf hear, the dumb speak, the lame walk, folk suffering from fevers are cured, the lepers are cleansed, those possessed of the devil are freed . . .

John of Salisbury, 1171

It would be surprising if none of those cures happened. Sick people often cure themselves with a short holiday. A friend can encourage a person with arthritis to do a little walking. In the middle ages some people became violent (or, they believed, 'possessed by the devil') after eating infected bread. A few days walking with friends to a shrine and eating different food could have worked wonders in days when most people believed in miracles.

Many pilgrims visited a shrine to do penance for sins. A penance worked like a forfeit. A man or woman confessed their sins to a priest who said that forgiveness would come if they did a penance such as going without food, saying extra prayers or going on a pilgrimage.

Probably the main reason for a pilgrimage was that people believed that it was their duty to God to make at least one pilgrimage in their life. It was all the better if the place they went to had relics, or remains, connected with saints or even the life of Christ Himself.

11 Relics were put in reliquaries which were richly carved caskets like this.

1 Describe the scene on the side of the reliquary. What sorts of relics may it have held?
2 How would this casket have been like the one made to hold the arm of St Jerome (source 12)?

The main tourist route for foreign pilgrims ⟩⟩

1 Canterbury Cathedral – St Thomas Becket
2 Bury St Edmunds Abbey – King Edmund, killed by Vikings
3 Ely Cathedral – St Ethelreda who started the monastery
4 Norwich Cathedral – St William, a murdered boy
5 Walsingham Abbey – a statue of Our Lady with great healing powers
6 Bromholm Abbey – a piece of the true cross
7 Lincoln Cathedral – St Hugh, a bishop
8 Durham Cathedral – St Cuthbert, a monk of Saxon times
9 York Cathedral – St William, an archbishop
10 Lichfield Cathedral – St Chad, a Saxon bishop
11 Worcester Cathedral – St Oswald, a Norman bishop, and St Wulstan, a Saxon bishop
12 Malmesbury Abbey – St Aldhelm, the founder of the abbey
13 Glastonbury Abbey – St Joseph of Arimathea
14 Salisbury Cathedral – St Osmund, a Norman bishop
15 Winchester Cathedral – St Swithin, a Saxon bishop

12 The leading shrines and relics.

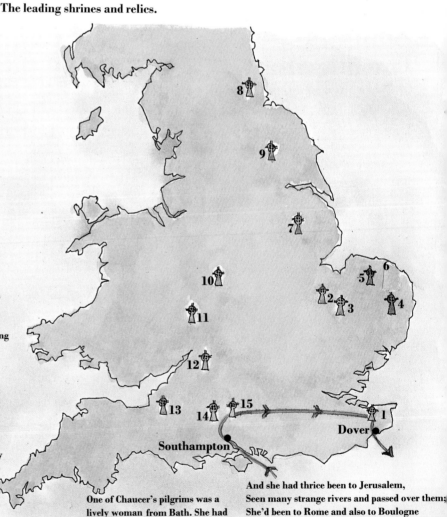

One of Chaucer's pilgrims was a lively woman from Bath. She had been married five times and travelled a great deal:

And she had thrice been to Jerusalem,
Seen many strange rivers and passed over them;
She'd been to Rome and also to Boulogne
St James of Compostella and to Cologne.
The Canterbury Tales, *Prologue*

Matthew Paris, was a monk in St Albans Abbey who wrote books about history and the church. He described Abbot William who never missed a chance to collect another relic:

> **12** When he attended the translation [saint-making ceremony] of St Wulstan . . . he obtained one of his ribs for us . . .
> Abbot William also acquired for us . . . an arm of St Jerome, which he enclosed in superbly-made goldsmith's work embellished with gems. This was carried round at special festivities . . .
>
> Matthew Paris, *Chronicle*, around 1240

13 A badge which shows that the pilgrim had been to Canterbury.

A journey to Canterbury

Pilgrims often travelled in parties as tourists do today. The poor went on foot, carrying their belongings in a sack tied to a stick or stave. The well-to-do could afford to travel on horseback and stay in inns.

When they came to Canterbury they would find the streets crowded with other pilgrim parties. There were town laws to stop pilgrims being pestered:

> **14** No Inn Keeper or Host, when any pilgrims or strangers come to the city shall catch them by their reins, or their staves and try to make them come into his Inn . . . under pain of imprisonment or fine.

So many pilgrims went into Canterbury Cathedral that monks had to control the traffic. A monk met each party at the door in the north transept and told them to get into a line. He then led them to the Altar of the Sword's Point – the actual spot where St Thomas Becket had been killed. After they had prayed the guide led them along the aisles behind the choir stalls. This could have been the first time that they had ever been in the eastern part of a cathedral. Very likely they were told not to make any noise which would interrupt the choir or a priest saying mass in a chantry chapel.

The guide led them up some steps on to the Trinity Chapel behind the high altar. At the top they came to St Thomas' shrine. The monk told them to kneel. You can still see where their knees have worn the tiles. He pulled on a rope which lifted the wooden cover from the shrine to show the plates of gold loaded with diamonds, emeralds, sapphires and rubies. The pilgrims would pray or just gaze in wonder until it was time to give way to the next group.

Afterwards the pilgrims were expected to leave an offering. One important reason for having a good show of relics was to encourage pilgrims to visit your cathedral or abbey. The top places of pilgrimage were able to pay for new buildings out of the money they collected.

3 The figure above is Thomas Becket. How would you know he was an archbishop?

4 What might be a present-day version of this badge?

5 Design a notice or poster which explains the town law in source 14.

6 Match these terms with their definitions. Five are left for you to do:

rood screen   Lady chapel
chantry   misericord
shrine   reliquary
sanctuary   mass
choir

A place of worship dedicated to Christ's mother

A tomb containing the body of a saint

The part of the church where the hours were sung

A service which commemorated the Last Supper

15 Pillars.

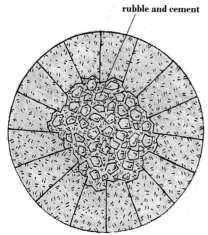

rubble and cement

Round Norman pillars. Masons had only axes to shape the stones. The outer stones did not fit together tightly so the strength of the pillar came from the rough stones and cement in the centre.

single piece of stone

marble

Gothic pillars. Masons had chisels to cut the stones into exact shapes so they could lock them together. The rubble in the centre was not needed. The masons could also use chisels to carve columns on the outside. The black marble columns were added later for decoration only.

16 Buttresses.

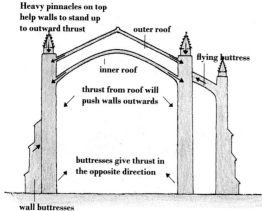

Heavy pinnacles on top help walls to stand up to outward thrust

outer roof

flying buttress

inner roof

thrust from roof will push walls outwards

buttresses give thrust in the opposite direction

wall buttresses

In the streets outside, the travellers would be jostled by street traders trying to sell them pilgrim's badges to hang from their shoulder sack or their horse's saddlebag.

New buildings, new styles

Look at the picture of Lincoln's nave on page 36 and compare it with the nave at Durham on page 15. Durham was one of the last cathedrals to be built in the Norman style. Lincoln's nave was an example of a new style, the Gothic.

---

1 Make notes about the main differences between a Norman and a Gothic building under these headings:

a The shape and size of pillars

b The shape and height of arches

c The way the triforium is divided

d The design and size of the clerestory

e Ways of adding decoration

The Gothic style came to Europe in the mid 1100s when crusaders came back from wars in the Arab lands and described the pointed buildings they had seen there. It first came to England in the 1180s just after the east end of Canterbury Cathedral had burned to the ground. The monks chose a Frenchman to make a much larger east end in the new style. After that priests and monks changed to the new style whenever they had the money to rebuild part of their cathedral or abbey church.

How did they stand up?

The new buildings were much taller than Norman ones. They had massive roofs with towers and spires which could be seen for miles. Yet, inside, the pillars are slender and there often seems to be hardly any solid wall. How did they stand up? The diagrams on this page will show you.

The English Gothic styles

The Gothic styles lasted in Britain from just before 1200 to around 1500. There are special terms to describe whether a building comes from the beginning, middle or end of the Gothic period.

17 Vaults.

1. Barrel vaults can be found in early Norman churches. When the key stones are in place the vault cannot collapse.

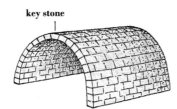

key stone

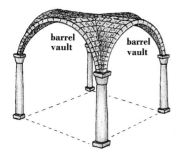

barrel vault   barrel vault

light stones

2. Cross-vaults soon followed. Two sections of a barrel vault could cover a square space.

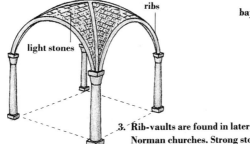

ribs

3. Rib-vaults are found in later Norman churches. Strong stone ribs were put up first. Then the spaces were filled with lighter stones.

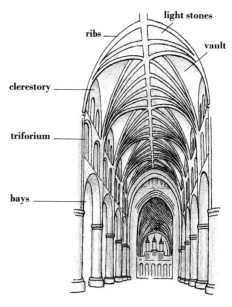

light stones

ribs

vault

clerestory

triforium

bays

4. Vaults in Gothic churches had pointed ribs. They could be used to cover large spaces like the nave at Lincoln.

18 Early English: about 1180s to about 1280s

Lincoln   South-east transept

19 Decorated: about 1280s to about 1350s

Lincoln   Angel Choir

20 Perpendicular: about 1350s to early 1500s

Gloucester Choir looking east

---

1 Make up a simple guide, with sketches, to the three styles. You could divide it into windows, pillars and arches, and wall decorations.

2 Look up the meaning of 'perpendicular' in a dictionary. Are 'decorated' and 'perpendicular' helpful descriptions?

3 Invent another name for Early English which is more helpful to recognising the style.

4 Look at the Lady Chapel at Lichfield (page 39). Which style is it?

5 What can you learn about the beliefs of people in the middle ages from the way they built their cathedrals?

Review and Assessment

21 Part of the nave and the south transept of Winchester Cathedral.

1 Look at this picture of the nave of Winchester Cathedral.
  a What name do you give to the style of building used in a) the transept, and b) the nave?
  b Roughly how many years were there between the times when the two parts were built: 30, 50, 100, 200, 300 or 500?
  c Explain how you have worked out your answer.

2 Winchester was a monastery-cathedral.
  a Imagine you are standing in the nave 500 years ago. Describe the activities you would see and hear.
  b What buildings would have been around Winchester cathedral in the middle ages?
  c Name four buildings in a secular cathedral close. Say who used each.

3 Look at these pictures:
  A A rood-screen – page 37
  B The Corpus Christi procession – page 37
  C Monks singing the hours – page 38
  D A priest saying Mass – page 38
  E A reliquary – page 40
  a With the help of these pictures write an account of the daily life of a cathedral priest or monk.
  b Explain how the pictures show that priests and monks had a special place in society.

4 **a** What did people of the middle ages believe about their souls and what happened to them after death?
  b How can we be helped to understand these ideas by:
    i)   The way that many new monasteries were started?
    ii) The money given for chantries?
    iii) The journeys made by pilgrims?

5 Look at what John of Salisbury said about the tomb of Thomas Becket (page 39)
  a Give reasons why it may have been easier to believe in miracles of this kind in the middle ages than it is today.
  b Would it be possible to understand the story of cathedrals if you did not accept that John of Salisbury believed in the truth of what he wrote?

The close and the monastery

1 A fourteenth-century painting of the bishop's palace and the cathedral in Wells.

1 Which is the bishop's palace?

2 Do you think he lived more like a priest or a baron? Why?

3 How is the cathedral cut off from the rest of the town?

Not all bishops' palaces had moats and walls with battlements and towers, but they were all separate from the cathedral and its grounds. This is because the bishop did not act as head of the cathedral. He was head of all the churches and priests in his diocese. Often he only went into the cathedral two or three times a year. This was usually to ordain new priests by laying his hands on their head.

A bishop could be away for months at a time on the king's affairs. When he had time in the diocese his main duty was to make a visitation of its churches. A visitation was like a baron's movement about his lands. The bishop travelled with a household and stayed at different castles, houses and monasteries. During the day, his household checked on the upkeep of church buildings, service books and the priests' robes, and whether villagers had paid all the money owing to the church.

The picture shows that the cathedral was also surrounded by walls and gates. All cathedrals and large abbey churches had a large walled area in the centre of the town. Inside the walls lived the men who served the cathedral or abbey church. If it was a secular cathedral, served by priests, this area was the close. If it was a monastery-cathedral or an abbey church, the wall went round the monastery grounds.

The secular cathedral and its close

The artist did not give a true picture of the size of the close at Wells. You can get a better idea from the plan, on page 46, of the close at Lincoln as it was in the fourteenth century. It holds several churches and chantry buildings as well

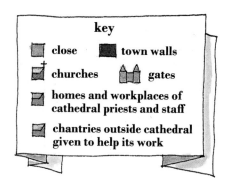

key
- close
- town walls
- churches
- gates
- homes and workplaces of cathedral priests and staff
- chantries outside cathedral given to help its work

2 A plan of Lincoln Cathedral close.

1 What does the plan tell you about the place of the bishop in running the cathedral?

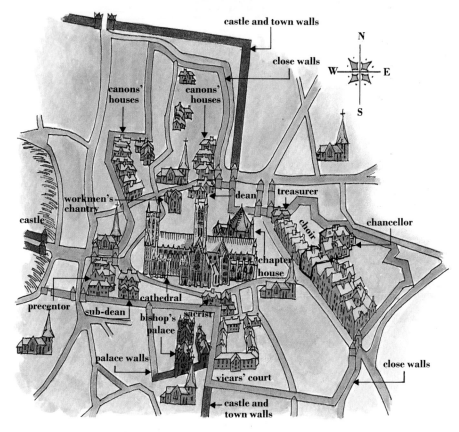

as the cathedral itself. There are also the homes and offices of the different priests who served the cathedral. During the day the gates were open so that townspeople and pilgrims could visit the cathedral. They were shut at night and when there was any trouble in the town.

Canons and vicars

We know how the cathedral got such a large piece of land for its close next to the castle. In about 1070 William the Conqueror issued a charter to the Bishop of Lincoln. Read the first part and answer the questions on the left:

2 Find Dorchester and Lincoln on the map on page 13. Why did William move the bishop's seat to Lincoln?

3 What does he mean by 'the mother church of the entire diocese'?

4 What does the charter mean by 'subsidiary buildings'?

3 Know that I have transferred the seat of the bishopric of Dorchester to the city of Lincoln with the authority and advice of Archbishop Lanfranc and the other bishops of my kingdom, and have given enough land there for building the mother church of the entire diocese and its subsidiary buildings.

Now read the second part of the charter:

4 Wishing also to make some grant to the same church for the salvation of my soul I give . . . the churches of three of my manors with land and tithes . . . I also grant the four churches of Bedford, Leighton Buzzard, Buckingham and Aylesbury.

So William gave seven churches to Lincoln. Other kings gave more until the cathedral had about fifty. How did it use these churches? William says he gives them with 'land and tithes'. Every family in the parish had to hand over a tithe (or a tenth) of all the food it grew to the church.

The tithes and other fees from each church became a living (money to live on) for one of the priests who were canons of the cathedral. Out of them the canon paid another priest a small wage to take charge of the parish work. This humbler priest was called a vicar, which is an old word meaning 'stand-in'.

In the close the canon had another stand-in, his vicar-choral. He stood in for the canon to sing the hours. Each close had a vicar's court where they lived in rooms and had their meals together in a common room.

The Dean and Chapter

The canons met each day to discuss cathedral business in the chapter house. (The name for this building was taken from the name of the place where monks held their daily meetings, see page 48.) This is why all the canons together are known as a chapter. The head of the chapter was the dean. To help him run the cathedral he neeeded a sub-dean and three other senior canons with special jobs.

The **precentor** took charge of the cathedral services. He arranged the timetable of psalms and other music which the vicars – choral sang, helped by choirboys. He ran the practices of new music and the rehearsals for the priests and boys who would take part in special feast-day processions.

The **sacrist** was in charge of the church building and the people who worked there. He had a team of full-time maintenance workers such as carpenters and masons. He was also in charge of cleaners and people to look after the candle lighting. A sacrist often bought half a tonne of wax each year to be made into candles. He also ran a workshop for making the richly coloured vestments of the priests. His office was known as the sacristy and it had a strong room for storing the gold and silver plates, cups and crosses used in services.

The **chancellor** had two branches of work. First, he was in charge of all the cathedral's money and legal matters. Like the baron's chaplain he had clerks to write out letters and keep records. The chancellor also looked after the cathedral's schools and library.

All cathedrals had a choir school for boys to be trained in music, with some reading and writing as well. They also had grammar schools where boys came to study Latin. The grammar school was the starting point for going on to be a priest, or to work in the king's government or a baron's household.

Every cathedral had a collection of books used in services, copies of the Bible and writings about Christianity.

5 How do the plan and the information about people who worked in the close help to explain why Lincoln grew into one of the largest towns in the middle ages?

5 The library at Hereford Cathedral.

6 What does this tell you about the value of the books?

7 Inside Lincoln's chapter house. Like other chapter houses this was often used for great public events and important trials. King Edward 1 held one of the first parliaments here in 1301.

1 What does the layout of the chapter house suggest about how the room was used?

2 Which Gothic style is this?

The monastery and its grounds

The reconstruction opposite shows the grounds of St Albans Abbey. St Albans did not become a cathedral until the nineteenth century but monastery-cathedrals like Canterbury or Durham were set in grounds like these.

Notice how the monastery, like the close, takes up a large area with the townspeople's houses huddled outside the walls. Every day many of them came through the gateway to work as cooks, gardeners, bakers, brewers, stablemen, carpenters, labourers and handymen.

The monks' first duty was to sing the hours in the choir. In the daytime they went in procession from the cloisters. At 2 or 3 am they went down the night stairs in a sleepy file wearing fur-lined boots to deaden the sound and keep out the cold. The rood screen (see page 37) hid these comings and goings from people in the nave.

Each morning the monks met in the chapter house. In charge was the prior who ran the monastery and cathedral as the abbot's second in command. He had the same duties as the dean in a secular cathedral. The meeting began with reading a chapter from the Rule of St Benedict, which is where the name 'chapter house' comes from. After the chapter the monks went off to their work. Some would be excused singing the hours because they were obedientiaries with special jobs, like those done by the senior canons

The cloister and the scriptorium

Most monasteries had some monks who spent their life studying and writing. Matthew Paris was a monk at St Albans in the thirteenth century who wrote chronicles about the great events of his day. He would have worked at a wooden desk in the cloister. Sometimes he would have gone into the parlour (or talking room) where monks could speak to outsiders. Important visitors would have been glad to give him the latest news about the government or rows between the king and barons.

8 A reconstruction of St Albans Abbey grounds in the fourteenth century. Today only the cathedral and the gatehouse are still standing. A park, shops and houses cover the orchards and gardens, the monks' cemetery, the bakehouse and brewery, the stables and animal sheds.

9 The cloisters at Gloucester Abbey (now a cathedral) were built in about 1420. The spaces on the left were for monk's desks.

1 The design of the roof is called a fan-vault. Why do you think it has that name?

Books were made in the scriptorium or writing room. Each person in the scriptorium had a special skill. The work began with the monks who cut and smoothed calf's skin to make vellum or sheep's skin to make parchment.

A scribe (Latin for 'writer') wrote on the skins with a goose quills which he kept sharp with his knife. He first ran a wheel with sharp points down each side. This left tiny holes which he joined up with faint lines. He had to write in a standard script so it would be difficult to see where one monk had finished and another carried on.

Scribes left spaces for the illuminators. They decorated the capital letters and sometimes drew in the margins. Every now and then they would paint a small picture. It might be a scene from everyday life or it might tell of some important event. These manuscript pictures help us to understand life in the middle ages in the same way as a collection of photographs can illustrate our own century.

10 The words and music for services on St David's Day from a fourteenth-century book.

11 A picture from a manuscript of 1285. It shows King Edward I. He had just returned from the crusades and holds a sword. He is talking to two bishops who are wearing mitres on their heads and carry croziers (shepherd's crooks). Some of their household are behind them. The three figures at the bottom are priests who are working as clerks to note down what is agreed. Less important people were often painted small in pictures of this time.

One monk was an expert in making paints for the illuminator. His blue came from the indigo plant grown in India, green was made from copper mixed with the juice of rotten apples and yellow was saffron which was taken from crocuses.

The abbot

12 John Stoke, Abbot of At Albans.

1 Compare this with the picture of the Bishop of Wells in his palace (page 45). List the clues that tell us that abbots had the same social position as bishops.
2 Suggest what the abbot is holding in his left hand.
3 Use the picture to explain the meaning of crozier and mitre.
4 Draw a strip cartoon to explain the work of each of these people: sacrist; vicar-choral; chronicler; scribe.
5 Suppose you were thinking about a career 600 years ago and you had done well in your studies at grammar school. List the reasons for and against becoming a monk.

Like a bishop the abbot spent most of his life away from his abbey church. This could be because he was also the bishop if it was a monastery-cathedral. Abbots were also often judges or officials in the government. Like bishops they were great landowners. In the picture the abbot is holding a document with a large wax seal. It is a charter which gives proof that he has been granted something valuable. It could be a piece of land or the right to collect fees from markets or tithes from a parish.

13 A monk who served Canterbury Cathedral painted his brother monks coming to kneel at the feet of St Benedict. The words behind his head say 'St Benedict, father of monks and leader'.

The Orders

The monks who served all the monastery-cathedrals, except Carlisle, belonged to the **Benedictine Order**. 'Order' is the name given to all the monks who followed the Rule of the same founder. About half the nuns in England were also Benedictines, but no monastery-cathedrals were served by nuns.

The **Augustinians** were regular canons. 'Regular' means that they lived according to a Rule in a monastery. 'Canons' tell us that they were also priests who went out from the monastery to take services and help the poor or sick. Henry I was the first Norman king to spread his rule to the far north-west of England. He had a cathedral built in Carlisle with Augustinians to serve it. Many barons gave the monasteries near their castles to Augustinians. The Augustinian abbeys at Bristol, Oxford and Southwark became cathedrals in modern times.

The **Cistercians** were an important Order in Britain. They built huge abbeys in north England, Wales and Scotland. Their Order was started by French monks who believed in a hard-working, simple life in wilder country away from the towns. So they played no part in the story of cathedrals.

14 Clearing the ground at Citeaux.

6 Give examples to show why cathedrals and monasteries were important to each of: education; jobs; government; the growth of towns.

Review and Assessment

1 **Describe and explain with the help of evidence in Chapters 4 and 5**

a Four ways in which cathedrals have changed inside and outside since the middle ages.

b Why cathedrals had (i) a rood screen, (ii) chantries, and (iii) shrines.

c The differences between (i) a secular and a monastery-cathedral, (ii) the nave and the rest of the cathedral, and (iii) Norman and Gothic buildings.

d Which of these are facts and which are points of view:

nearly everyone in the middle ages believed in heaven and hell

people of the middle ages all led good lives

Gothic cathedrals were more beautiful than Norman ones

the word 'holiday' comes from 'holy day'

e How the artist who drew the picture on page 45 shows that the bishop is an important man.

2 **For each of these you first need to find the pages in Chapters 1 to 5 which give you the information and evidence.**

a Explain what was similar and what was different in:

(i) the life of a Benedictine and Cistercian monk

(ii) the appearance of a Norman and a Gothic cathedral

(iii) Dover Castle and Chepstow Castle

b The appearance of castles and cathedrals both began to change a lot in the years between the 1180s and the early 1200s. Give two reasons for the changes in castles and two for the changes in cathedrals.

c Explain the connections between each of these triplets:

tiltyard – melée – tournament

chapter-house – dean – sacrist

D-shaped tower – barbican – machicolation

mal-voisin – mangonel – trebuchet

Early English – Decorated – Perpendicular

d Think of a film which shows life in castles. Write a letter to the producer saying whether you think he has given a full picture of what castles were used for. Give your reasons.

e Imagine it is 1400 and *either* you are standing in a cathedral with a cousin from a country manor *or* you work as a servant in Chepstow Castle and your cousin comes to work there. Explain what goes on inside and around the cathedral or castle. Show how you could illustrate your account with pictures or quotations.

Wales and Scotland

The Welsh Marches

1 The Welsh are light and active, hardy rather than strong, and entirely bred up to the use of weapons. When the trumpet sounds the alarm, the farmer rushes as eagerly from the plough as the courtier from the court.

Gerald of Wales, *A Description of Wales*, 1194

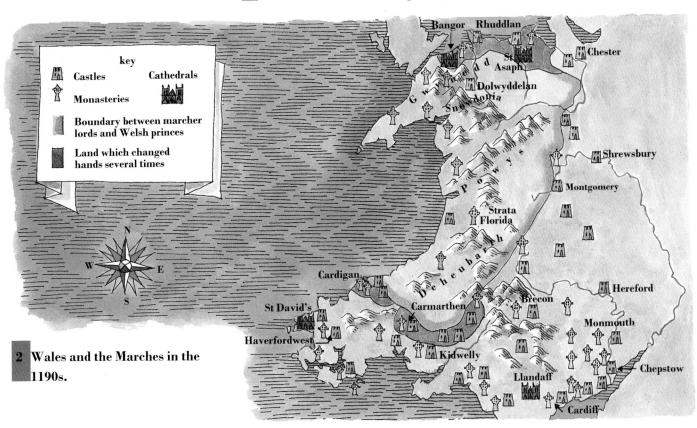

key

Castles   Cathedrals

Monasteries

Boundary between marcher lords and Welsh princes

Land which changed hands several times

Bangor   Rhuddlan

Chester

St Asaph

Dolwyddelan

Gwynedd

Snowdonia

Shrewsbury

Powys

Montgomery

Strata Florida

Cardigan

Deheubarth

Hereford

St David's

Carmarthen

Brecon

Haverfordwest

Monmouth

Kidwelly

Llandaff

Chepstow

Cardiff

2 Wales and the Marches in the 1190s.

Look at the map on page 55.

1 Why had the marcher lords conquered more of the south than the north?
2 Who would have brought the monasteries to Wales?
3 What differences would the coming of a castle or monastery have made to the life of a farming family in the area? Suggest reasons they might have for a) welcoming the castle, and b) being angry about it.

3 A picture from a thirteenth-century Welsh manuscript.

1 Welsh warriors must have had a good reason for wearing one shoe. What might it have been?
2 Look at sources 1–4 on pages 55 and 56. Say how each of them helps to explain why the English had not captured all of Wales.

The Normans had found it much harder to conquer the Welsh than the English. Welsh farmers' homes were scattered over the hills where their animals grazed. They were freemen who were not forced to work in their lord's fields. Yet each family had a lord and would fight alongside him whenever he called on them to bring their bows and spears.

William the Conqueror made special arrangements to deal with the Welsh. He chose three Normans to be earls of Chester, Shrewsbury and Hereford. The land on the borders of England and Wales was called the Marches and they were the marcher earls. The knights who served these earls were marcher lords. William expected them to fight their way into Wales and build castles as centres of Norman rule. Marcher lords were the only ones allowed to build castles without the king's permission.

There were more than a hundred smaller castles, not shown on the map, which were only a single stone tower or a motte and bailey. The land around one of these simple castles was a copy of life on a manor in England. The village people were no longer freemen but villeins who held land from the lord of the manor and paid him rent and other dues.

The marcher lords used the church to spread English ways into Wales. There were four cathedrals and the bishops had to accept the Archbishop of Canterbury as their primate. Many marcher lords gave land to English abbeys to open monasteries close to their castles. The monks helped the spread of English language and writing through the marches. The marcher lords looked on Welsh speaking, story telling and music as a mark of being less civilised.

Beyond the Marches

West of the Marches, Welsh princes ruled the land. At times their warriors defeated the English and took marcher castles. In the north they used these castles to help them to hold on to the lands they won.

Gerald warned the English about the risks of using soldiers on horseback to fight the Welsh. The Welsh fought on foot but they were tough and knew the mountains well, so they were able to ambush marcher soldiers. Their weapons looked crude but they were deadly.

A marcher baron described to Gerald what happened when one of his knights came up against the short bow:

4 Another soldier was likewise hit by an arrow which penetrated through his hauberk and leg armour and into his saddle. When he reined his horse round . . . a second arrow hit him in the other thigh so he was firmly fixed to his horse on both sides. What more could you expect, even from a crossbow?

Gerald of Wales, *The Journey Through Wales*, 1191

Wales and Edward I

In the thirteenth century the princes of Gwynedd rose to become leaders of all north and west Wales. The centre of their lands was the great mountain stronghold of Snowdonia. The new power of Gwynedd was the work of two princes, Llywelyn ap Iorweth and his grandson Llywelyn ap Gruffydd.

Llywelyn ap Gruffydd forced King Henry III to sign a treaty which said that the English accepted him as the Prince of Wales. In return Henry ordered Llywelyn to kneel and pay homage to him as his king.

In 1272 Henry III died and his son became King Edward I. Edward was away fighting in a crusade. When he came home in 1274 he knew more about castles than any king in Europe. In the Holy Land he had seen the massive castles which crusaders built. On his way he had seen the greatest new castles in France, Spain and Italy.

Edward ordered Llywelyn to come to England to pay homage to him. Three times Llywelyn refused. In 1276 Edward told his great council that he would crush Llywelyn who was 'a rebel and disturber of the peace'.

In July 1277 Edward marched from Chester at the head of 800 knights, 15,000 foot soldiers, 370 archers and a few thousand labourers. Close to the shore were twenty-five ships with the army's supplies. They left 3,000 labourers behind to build a castle at Flint and Edward then led his men and ships to Anglesey. Llywelyn's stronghold in Snowdonia was surrounded. He surrendered and agreed to do homage to Edward I and hand over the lands along the coast.

Edward needed the strongest possible castle to control the land that Llywelyn had given up. He decided it should be at Rhuddlan and put one of Europe's leading experts on castles in charge of the work. The English knew him as Master James.

3 In earlier chapters you have studied a) how castles were important for defence and as centres of government, and b) how monasteries were important to the social life of England. How does the story of Wales show the same importance for castles and abbeys there?

4 With the help of 1, 2 and 3 on the plan, explain how Rhuddlan is an example of a concentric castle.
5 Would it be possible to mine this castle?
6 Why would Master James be confident that the castle could stand up to a long siege by Welsh soldiers?
7 Check with the map on page 55 to explain why Edward I saw Rhuddlan as the key to keeping Llywelyn bottled up in Snowdonia.

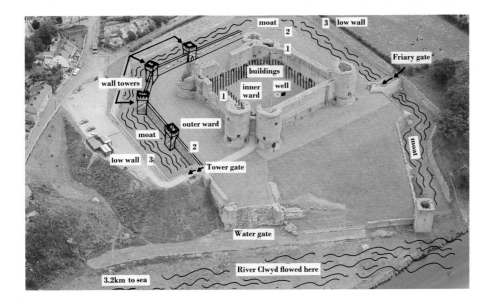

5 Rhuddlan Castle from the air.

1 **What would Edward have in mind when he planned the position of the new castles, shown on the map below?**

2 **Why were the strongest all close together in the north-west?**

3 **It took around two hundred years for the marcher lords to take control of half of Wales and only ten for Edward 1 to conquer the rest. Suggest some reasons for this.**

Most of Rhuddlan was finished by 1282. That was just as well because in that year Llywelyn and his brother Dafydd called their people to war against the English. The war went on until the middle of 1283. By then Llywelyn had been killed and Dafydd taken prisoner.

Edward was now master of Wales and intended to stay in control. He wiped Gwynedd from the map and divided it into counties with English names such as Caernarvonshire. The Welsh names were only given back to the present-day counties in 1974.

To keep the counties under English rule, Edward ordered barons to build new castles or strengthen their old ones. He also set Master James to work on four great royal castles at Conwy, Caernarfon, Harlech and Beaumaris. Beside each castle, James was told to build walls and towers to protect a new town. No Welsh would be allowed to live in these towns. They would be home for English tax collectors and other royal officials, judges, and people such as merchants and craftsmen.

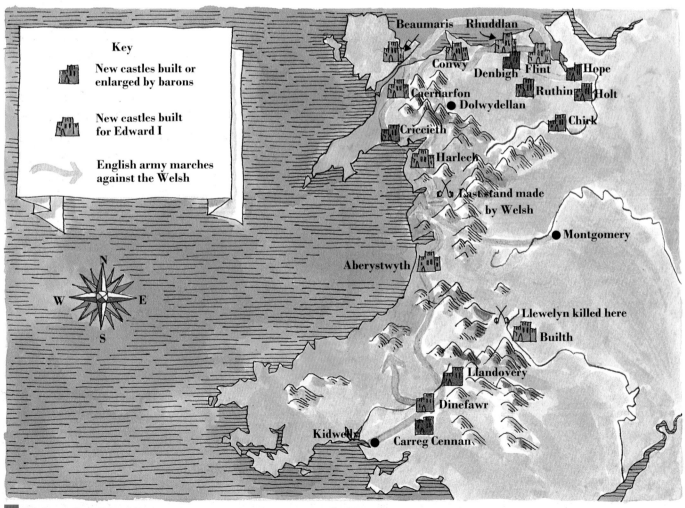

Key

New castles built or enlarged by barons

New castles built for Edward I

English army marches against the Welsh

6 Wales under Edward I.

Conwy and Caernarfon

7 Reconstruction of Conwy. The castle that Master James built as it would have looked just after it was finished, with its walls painted white. The inner ward (on the left) held apartments for the king and queen to stay in. The constable lived in two towers in the outer ward. The building on the rear wall is the great hall.

4 There was often only a small number of archers on castle-guard. How would it be possible for them to defend Conwy Castle?

5 Find the gateway into the outer ward. There is a barbican in front of it.
  a What does barbican mean?
  b How did this barbican help the defence of the castle?

6 Who was in charge of building the town defences at Conwy?

7 Why would English officials and settlers feel safe here?

8 Which do you think would be more important to English rule in Wales: the town or the castle? Why?

8 Plan of Conwy. It took only five years to build Conwy Castle and town walls. This picture shows the walls around 1600. The artist did not bother to show the buildings in the castle but he drew the town defences quite accurately. Most still stand today.

Caernarfon Castle took thirty years to finish. It was larger and more splendid than the others because it was the headquarters of the royal government in Wales. Edward had seen the city walls of Constantinople when he travelled to the Holy Land and ordered Master James to copy their bands of different coloured stone and polygonal towers.

9 **Caernarfon Castle as it looks today.**

1 Use this picture of Caernarfon to explain what polygonal means.
2 In 1404, twenty-eight men held out in the castle against a large Welsh army led by Owain Glendwr. How were they able to do this?
3 What impression would the castle have made on the conquered people of Wales?

Castles and cathedrals in Scotland

Scotland was a separate kingdom, but by Edward I's time its kings had ruled by Norman methods for 150 years. They began with David I (1124–53) who invited barons from England and Normandy to settle in Scotland. He gave them lands where they built motte and bailey castles. David and later kings also built castles in places where they stayed as they moved about with their households. Many were linked to walled towns which the Scots called burghs.

Most of the biggest castles were on rocks looking over roads and river crossings. The most important was Stirling. Many years later a writer said that Stirling was like a brooch which pinned the north and south of Scotland together. Any army moving between the two halves had to cross the river Forth near the hill where Stirling Castle perched.

Like the Normans in England the Scottish kings had a great respect for the church. They had eleven cathedrals built. The largest was St Andrews which was served by Augustinian canons. There were also many Benedictine monasteries and in the 1130s Cistercian monks arrived from Engand.

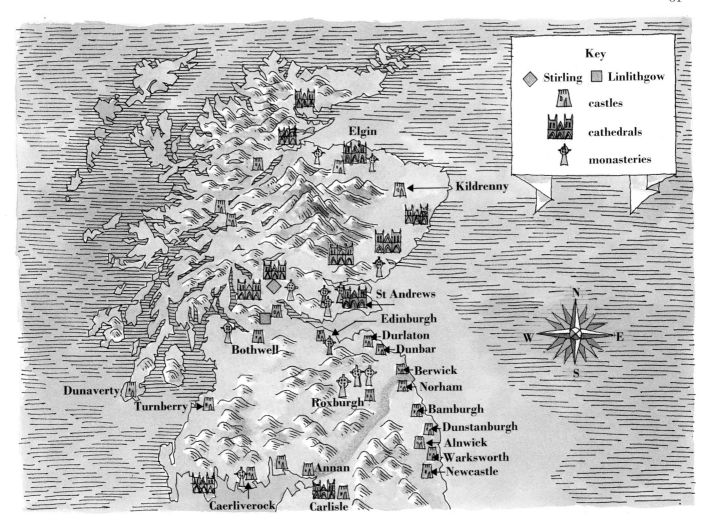

10 Scotland at the time of Edward I.

Edward I in Scotland

By 1290 Edward I had conquered Wales. Now he had a chance to become powerful in Scotland. The king of Scotland was killed when he was thrown from his horse. Thirteen Scottish lords claimed the right to become the new king. The Bishop of St Andrews asked Edward to make a choice. In 1291 he decided on John Balliol.

Edward then asked the grateful John Balliol to do homage to him as his overlord. The manuscript picture on page 62 shows that he did so.

Edward soon began to interfere in the way Balliol ruled Scotland, and ordered him to send soldiers to join the English army. Balliol refused. Edward did just as he had when Llywelyn stood up to him. He gathered a huge army and invaded.

Wars went on for most of the next thirty years. Scotland's castles held the key to whether English or Scottish kings ruled there. Four times the most important question was who held Stirling Castle, or who could find a way past it. Look out for these stories as you read about the wars.

4 Most of the castles on the map above were held by the king. How would they have been important to a) ruling the country, and b) defending it from invaders?

5 How would you describe the position of the cathedrals and monasteries?

6 What would be the main purpose of the castles on the English side of the border?

11 John Balliol doing homage to Edward I.

1 How does this picture explain the meaning of 'doing homage'?

Edward and Wallace, 1296–1305

Edward began by capturing Berwick. To give a taste of what would come his soldiers slaughtered the townspeople. Afterwards, they swept along the line of castles on the east of Scotland. It took just three days of battering from siege engines to get Edinburgh to surrender. News of what had happened at Berwick and Edinburgh reached the garrison at Stirling. They fled.

Edward captured every castle as far north as Elgin. Then he took his army back to England leaving each castle with a garrison of English soldiers and officials. The people of the countryside would not obey the English in the castles. Many joined the army of a Scottish lord, William Wallace. In a year Wallace had captured back the castles north of Stirling. The English sent another army. They met at Stirling at the bridge over the river Forth.

The Scots waited until part of the English army were across and then attacked the English knights before they could get their horses on the move. Many English were killed. The rest scattered. Edward took his army away.

In 1303, Edward took another army to Scotland. This time he planned to get round Stirling. He had parts for three floating bridges towed up the North Sea. His troops used them to cross the river Forth a safe distance from Stirling and then they marched on to capture all the castles they had taken in 1296.

While they were marching north Edward had time to besiege Stirling Castle. Thirteen siege engines hurled stones uphill at its walls. At the end of this invasion the English captured Wallace, took him to London and put him to a cruel death.

Robert Bruce fights back, 1306–14

Robert Bruce was a Scottish Earl. In 1306 the Bishop of Glasgow crowned him king. For two years he had to keep on the move, fleeing from the English soldiers. In 1307 Edward I died and his son became King Edward II.

Gradually Bruce built up a new Scots army. It had no siege engines. Yet the daring of his followers helped Bruce to capture the castles one by one.

At Linlithgow a farmer hid Bruce's men in hay he was delivering to the castle. He jammed the cart in the gateway. The fighters leapt out and overpowered the guards. At Edinburgh they found a soldier whose sweetheart was a servant in the castle. He led soldiers up a secret path he used to visit her. At Roxburgh, Bruce's men, wrapped in cloaks, crept towards the castle on all fours at dusk. The guards thought they were cattle until they produced ladders and climbed the wall. At Bothwell the attackers crossed the moat where it was only deep enough to come up to a man's chin.

Bruce knew that the castles were the only way that the English could control Scotland. So when he had taken a castle, he had it destroyed. By 1314 Stirling was the only important castle left in English hands. Bruce's army surrounded it. Edward II sent an army to break up the Scots' siege.

12 A fifteenth-century drawing of the Battle of Bannockburn.

13 The Battle of Bannockburn.

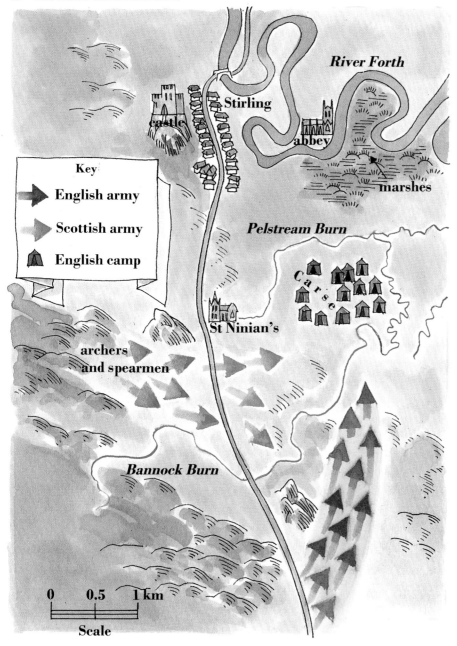

Key
→ English army
→ Scottish army
⛺ English camp

River Forth

Stirling
castle
abbey
marshes

Pelstream Burn

Carse

St Ninian's

archers
and spearmen

Bannock Burn

0   0.5   1 km
Scale

2   How does this map explain the importance of Stirling Castle?

3   What could have happened if the English had won the Battle of Bannockburn?

4   Use the map to explain what happened at Stirling in 1297.

5   How did Edward I get past Stirling in 1303?

6a How does the picture on page 62 give different information from the map?

 b Could the artist of the picture have had a reason for showing the battle so close to the town and castle?

 c What impression does he give of the difference between the English and Scots armies?

7   How were castles in Wales and Scotland similar as a way of controlling a) local people, and b) important routes.

8   Explain whether you think there are any similarities between the importance of Rhuddlan and Stirling castles.

Bruce was waiting with an army of about 5,000. The English had to go downhill and to the right to avoid them. They ended up on the carse (or meadow) between the Bannock Burn and the Pelstream Burn. There they spent the night.

Next morning the Scots advanced on the English. The English archers and knights had no room to get into fighting positions.

The result was a complete victory for the Scots. Now they could take Stirling, the last important castle in English hands.

Pele towers

The Battle of Bannockburn ended the English hopes of ruling Scotland. But it did not stop fighting between the followers of lords on each side of the border, which went on through the fourteenth and fifteen centuries. Bands of armed men crossed the border from each side to steal cattle and leave farms in smoking ruins.

To protect themselves, farmers and villagers built pele towers. Pele comes from the old word for pale which means a fence or wall. Most of the walls have disappeared but there are hundreds of pele towers on each side of the border. Some stand in lonely places on the moors but many have been made into part of a farm or house.

14 A tower built into a modern home. The wall in front may have been part of the fourteenth-century pele.

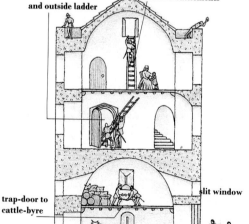

15 A cross-section of a pele tower in south Scotland.

1 Study the diagram.
a Which is the only way in?
b What are the men on the first floor doing?
c What does the diagram tell us about the date of the window in the photograph?
2 Does the tower in the photograph have machicolation?
Explain your answer.
3 Describe the ways in which a pele tower and a keep like the one at Hedingham (page 20) are a) similar, and b) different.
4 Pele towers are much simpler than square keeps yet they came 300 years later. How would you explain that?

Review and Assessment

1 Make a time chart of what Edward I was doing in these years:
1272–74, 1277–83, 1291, 1296, 1303–5

2 Edward I called Llywelyn 'a rebel and a disturber of the peace'. Was this a fact or was it Edward's point of view? Explain your answer.

3 Most English people's evidence about Wales in the middle ages comes from the writings of Gerald of Wales and from castles built by the English.

a What impression of the Welsh do you get from such evidence?

b In which ways might it not give a complete picture of Welsh people?

c What sorts of evidence might be used to give a more accurate view?

4 These two accounts are taken from different school books:

a It was during these long hard years of struggle that the Scots began to think of themselves as a 'nation'. The hardship which the people had to endure made them feel that all Scots had some things in common, such as history and their kings. The fact that they also felt that they had a common enemy in the English additionally helped on the idea of Scots nationhood.
Ian Ferguson, 1987

b In 1287 a rebellion against the English broke out, led by William Wallace. The Scots were crushed again, Wallace caught and executed. A new leader, Robert Bruce, then rebelled and claimed the Scottish throne. His cause seemed hopeless because the English held important castles. But Bruce and the Scots did not give up, so when Edward died in AD1307 they were still fighting.
John Ray and James Hagerty, 1987

Which was written for a) Scottish, b) English schools? Explain how you decided.

5 **a** What idea is put forward in the first extract above which is not included in the way the story is told in this chapter?

b In the second extract the Scots are said to have broken out in 'rebellion' led by Wallace. In this chapter it says they 'joined the army of Wallace'. Suggest a reason why the author of this book did not use the word 'rebellion'.

c What is the difference between the words used to describe Wallace's death in the second extract and on page 62? Explain which words you would use.

6 Write your own summary (80–120 words) of the wars between England and Scotland. Add a paragraph to explain why you think it is a fairer account than each of the extracts in question 4.

7 Builders and decorators

1 A fourteenth-century building site.

1 What signs are there in this picture that the person in charge of the work had a high social position?
2 Which are the free masons, the laying masons and the labourers?
3 How does the picture help to explain why the person in charge was known as a 'master mason'?
4 What two ways of lifting materials can you see?
5 Make a sketch of what the laying mason is using instead of a spirit level.
6 Who do you think would be the better paid, the free masons or the laying masons? Why?

The important people in the picture above are those who are drawn the biggest. The king has his courtiers behind him. The man pointing is in charge of the work. The smaller figures are the building-site workers. There are two free masons who are shaping stones, two laying masons and two labourers.

Getting ready

The person in charge of building a castle or cathedral was the master mason. He or she had to be far more than just a skilled stone worker. The master mason designed the building and organised the work and pay of hundreds of masons and other craftsmen and labourers. There would be no work for him if he could not keep accounts and write in Latin and French.

When a king, baron or cathedral chapter wanted a new building they looked for a master mason who was good at the sort of design they had in mind. For his castles in Wales, Edward I chose Master James of St George. When the east end of Canterbury Cathedral burned down in 1174, the monks chose William of Sens, a master mason from Normandy. They wanted a new east end in the Gothic style which was just appearing in Europe.

A master mason would come only if his pay and conditions were right. Most expected to be paid about the same as a knight could earn from his manor. They wanted free, comfortable lodgings and, each year, a new fur-lined cloak of the sort that a king or baron gave to his highest household officials.

Once that was settled, the master mason would get to work. He made sketches of the building to show what was planned. Then he told carpenters to put up the site buildings. There would be large wooden shelters called lodges and a tracing house with a floor covered with the hardest kind of plaster which had to be imported from Paris. The master used the tracing floor to draw outlines of arches, windows and pillars. These gave the free masons the measurements they needed to start work in their lodge.

Masons had to cut hundreds of pieces of ashlar before building could begin. Ashlar is the name for stone which has been cut and smoothed so it can be used for the outside of walls and pillars.

2 This painting of a building site shows masons in a lodge and a master mason, or his assistant talking to a man mixing mortar.

7 Explain what the two people on the left are doing.

8 Suggest a use for the pieces of waste stone.

Sometimes the stone came from a local quarry which might be owned by the cathedral or abbey. But often the master mason bought it from far away. William of Sens bought his building stone from Caen in France. For decoration he ordered marble from Purbeck in Devon. When the stone came a long distance it was cut into rough shape before it was loaded on boats for its long trip by sea and river.

The second most important person on the building site was usually the master carpenter. His first job was to visit nearby woods to mark the trees to be cut down. When the wood was delivered his carpenters began to make scaffolding, arch supports and wheels to lift heavy stones and timbers. There were two kinds of wheel. A windlass, like the one in the picture opposite, had spokes so it could be turned by hand. For the heaviest objects a treadwheel was used. It needed the weight of two labourers who 'walked' inside it.

At work on the site

The first job was to make foundations. Where pillars were going to hold up a tower, the labourers often had to dig down to ten metres. Under walls they usually made a trench about a metre deep and filled it with rough stone.

The laying masons could then start using the ashlar cut in the lodge. They worked on walls and pillars at the same time so they would all reach the same height together. The diagram on page 42 shows how they used ashlar on the outside and packed the middle with rough stones, including the waste from the mason's lodge. If one stone was not exactly level the laying masons tilted it with a piece of oyster shell.

The walls and pillars would soon be too tall to work on from the ground. From this point the building would need teamwork between the masons and the carpenters.

An arch cannot stay up until the key stone at the centre of the top has been put in. So the carpenters had to make a centering frame and fit it on top of the pillars. Once the first arch of stones was in, the masons could use it to support arches of broader stones. The centering frame was taken away and used for the next arch.

When October came, outside work stopped. Frost would crumble the mortar so the tops of walls and pillars were covered with thick layers of straw or bracken to protect them (see the picture on page 67). After this there would be no work for the laying masons and most of the labourers. They were paid off and sent home. Some of the free masons and carpenters would be luckier. They could work on in the lodge cutting the stones and shaping the roof beams for next year's work.

3 A laying mason was often paid by the amount of work he had done in a week. When a section was finished he cut his own mark to be sure of his wages.

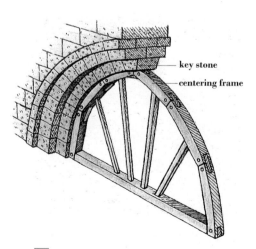

key stone

centering frame

4 Building an arch.

1 How would stones be lifted to the laying masons?

Towards heaven

Inside a cathedral you can look up at the vaults, but above them there is the roof that you see from the outside. This was always fitted before the vaulting by carpenters. They had to haul up massive timbers to start the roof framework. When the first beams were in place they would fit a treadwheel to lift the rest of the materials.

The carpenters worked like steeplejacks until the whole 'A' shaped frame was in position. The wood from hundreds of trees was needed to cover a nave and many of the beams were ten or more metres long. Once the frame was in place the carpenters covered it with planks. Then they handed over to plumbers who fitted sheets of lead over the planks to make the roof watertight. On the bottom edges they made lead gutters to collect the rainwater.

Today water runs down pipes into drains. In the middle ages it had to be made to fall to the ground clear of the buildings. So the masons made stone spouts, called gargoyles from the old French word for 'throat'.

When the roof was in place the vault could be put up, whatever the weather. A vault was usually made of stone. The masons first built it on the ground around centerings made by the carpenters. Then they numbered each piece and took it all apart. The treadwheel in the roof was used to lift the stones and centerings up. Then they were put back together again.

Sometimes a vault was made of timber. The builders decided this was the only safe way to cover the very wide nave in York Cathedral.

Spires are another example of the team work between masons and carpenters. The carpenters had to build a wooden frame before the masons put the stone work around it.

6 Gargoyles were one of the parts of a cathedral where masons were allowed free choice. They often carved fantastic figures like this.

7 This wall picture in Canterbury Cathedral was painted around 1280 and shows St Paul shaking off a viper.

8 The main strength of pointed vaults is in the ribs which were built first. In a vault the key stone is called a boss. Free masons were sent up to carve a head, leaves or a scene on the boss.

9 The west front of Wells Cathedral was built by a team of masons between around 1130 and 1143. People who have studied the work on the sculptures which are left, think that there were probably twelve sculptors in the team. Before the sixteenth century there were around 400 stone figures.

Decorators

Painters

The people who design buildings today are fond of letting you see stone, brick and wood in their natural state without plastering or painting. Builders in the middle ages would have thought this quite absurd. They had the west front of Wells Cathedral painted with the figures picked out in bright colours. Inside, walls were often painted too. Sometimes lines in red or black were painted to imitate the edge of stones.

Where there was a large wall space there was usually a painted picture showing scenes from the Bible or the lives of saints. Most have disappeared but in a few places they have been found under whitewash or plaster.

Sculptors

If you look at any Gothic building you will see many examples of stone carving such as the fine tracery work in windows and in choir screens. Also, there is often a lot of sculpture. Figures of people and animals were carved on roof bosses, and gargoyles and statues were often used to decorate walls. This tells us that some of the free masons were especially skilled at carving or sculpture. Often they were the finishers in a team of masons, putting the finishing touches to a piece of work. The less skilled ones first gave a rough shape to pieces of stone and then handed them over to the sculptors.

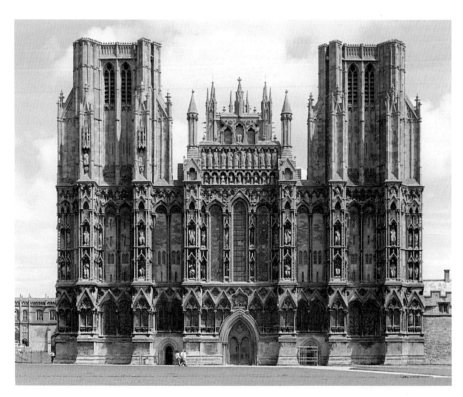

Monument makers

If you took up the floor of any cathedral you would find the bones of hundreds of bishops, noblemen, knights and merchants. Most of the places where their stone coffins lie are not known. They were once marked with a slab which has worn away or been covered by a later floor. But you can still see many tombs where the greatest and richest people were buried. Some are in chantry chapels and the others are usually in the aisles.

Most tombs are made up of three parts. The tomb itself is usually decorated. On top there is a carved effigy of the dead person. It may not be a good likeness because the sculptor may never have seen the person. In the middle ages effigies were always made to lie with their feet pointing to the east. Edward's feet rest on a lion but many other effigies show a dog. You can tell a person's position in society from the effigy. Kings and queens wear crowns, a bishop has his mitre and crozier and knights are usually shown in armour. Above the effigy there is usually a canopy carved in the style of the time.

10 People who were not as important as kings or bishops sometimes had their burial place under the floor marked with a brass memorial fitted on to a marble slab. Here a widow is watching engravers cut out the effigy of her dead husband with fine chisels. The lines will then be filled in with black pitch (a kind of tar). Sometimes brasses were coloured.

11 The tomb of King Edward II, who died in 1327, in Gloucester Cathedral.

Glaziers

In parts of Gothic cathedrals with large windows there was not much wall space to cover with pictures. So the work of glaziers, who made the stained glass, became more important in giving colour and richness.

Stained glass was not made on the site. It was bought from a glazier's workshop. First, the glazier made a full-sized colour design on a table. Then he or she sorted through the stock of different coloured glass sheets bought from a glass-house. The glazier then laid them over the plan and traced the outline with chalk. With a red-hot iron he scratched along the chalk marks so that the glass cracked and he could break off the unwanted bits to leave a piece that was the shape needed for his design.

When all the pieces were ready they were laid on the table and carefully joined with strips of lead. The complete window had to be packed in a box with hay and straw for its journey. If at all possible it would be taken by river to avoid jolting it on the rough cart tracks.

12 **A picture made just of coloured glass would have been very uninteresting. In this window from Canterbury Cathedral, the glazier had to paint in the shadow lines on Adam's ribs, hair and face, and the lines and dashes on the earth and grass. When the paint was dry the glass was put in a furnace where the heat fused the paint into the suface of the glass.**

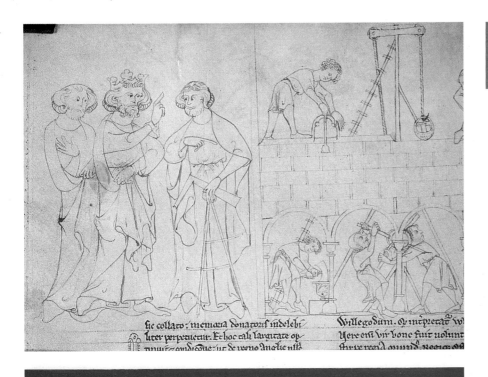

13 This drawing comes from one of Matthew Paris's books and shows building work on St Albans Abbey around 1250.

1 Look at the drawing above

a Who are the three tall figures on the left?

b What is the right-hand figure of these holding?

c What can we learn from the way he is dressed?

d On the building site, which are the two free masons and which are the two laying masons?

e What is the left man on top of the wall doing?

f If he found a mistake how could he put it right?

g What do you call the machine at the bottom? What was it for?

h How would the arches have been made to stand up?

i Name two other kinds of tradesmen who would been at work on building the abbey. What did each of them do?

j Why are the men on the left taller than those on the right?

OR

2 Make notes to go with this drawing to show how it can be used to explain how cathedrals and abbey churches were built in England and France. Add notes on important information about building methods and workers which are not in the picture.

3 Make up sentences which use each of these pairs: free mason / ashlar key stone / centering frame rib / boss lead / gargoyle effigy / canopy laying masons / put-log holes roof / vault carver / tracery stained glass / painted glass

8 The end of the story?

Castles

When is a castle not a castle?

1 Compare this with the picture of Caernarfon Castle on page 60. In which ways does this seem a) a true castle, and b) a grand home dressed up as a castle?

1 Herstmonceux Castle was built around 1440.

If you took a tour round England and Wales in 1440 you would have seen more ruins than standing castles. About 1,700 castles had been built in the two hundred years after the Norman conquest. Already more than half were no more than mounds of earth. They were the motte and baileys which never had stone work and some stone castles which had been pulled down by order of a king. You would also find many castles where the constable was only a caretaker, looking after a building which was never used.

This was because castles were no longer important to keeping the countryside peaceful. Barons did not act as local judges and tax collectors as they had done in the early middle ages. These jobs were done by the king's own judges who toured the country or by the king's sheriff and other officials in each county.

The poorer lords gave up living in castles and the greater ones usually chose one of their castles as their main home. Inside its strong walls, they built new halls, kitchens and lodgings for their household and the officers of their private armies. They were places like Warwick (page 29), Kenilworth (page 25), Caernarfon (page 60), Chepstow (page 29) and the king's own palace-castle at Windsor.

You would have seen a few new castles like Herstmonceux. From a distance you might think that it could stand a long siege. It had a deep moat, polygonal towers and machicolation. As you came near you would see that it was built of brick and that its windows were meant to let in light not keep out missiles.

Gunpowder

Why were castles no longer important in warfare? Some books tell you that it was because gunpowder had been invented in the early 1300s and castle walls could not stand up to cannon fire. Is there any evidence for this idea?
The most usual evidence that gunpowder could be used is that some castles had gun port-holes built into their gate-house towers in around 1400.

For about 150 years gunpowder was of more use to defenders than attackers. If you were rushing a gatehouse under a wooden screen you were protected from arrows but not from a cannon ball fired straight at you from fifty metres.

To be successful, attackers first had to make the castle walls crumble. This needed massive cannon. Around 1400 some had been made but they only fired stones. Trebuchets were still easier to make, cheaper and more powerful. It was only around 1450 that cannon could fire iron balls. They were tougher than stone so it was the walls which shattered, not the cannon-ball. In France you can see castles where a thick earth rampart was built behind the stone wall to take the shock of the cannon-ball. This was not done in England. New styles of fighting made it unnecessary.

2a How does the gunner use the slit above the port-hole?
b What is the second man doing?
3 Do the port-holes suggest that guns made castles easier or more difficult to defend?

2 Gun port-holes.

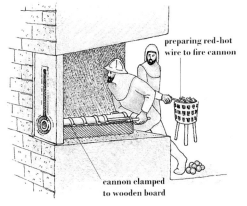

preparing red-hot wire to fire cannon

cannon clamped to wooden board

Commanders did not think it worth capturing castles and the few people in them. They tried to win battles in the open countryside. If they could kill many soldiers and capture their leaders it could be years before the enemy got another army together. In the Wars of the Roses between 1455 and 1485 there was only one siege – at Bamburgh Castle. The rest of the story is one of battles.

Slighting in the Civil War.

In 1642 King Charles I and Parliament went to war against each other. Parliament (led by Oliver Cromwell) had the largest and strongest armies and the king's supporters often took shelter in a castle. Parliament's armies then besieged them.

In the end the Royalists (who supported the king) almost always had to give in. Parliament then ordered the castle to be slighted.

Slighting was a cheaper way of making a castle impossible to live in than taking it apart stone by stone. Usually the slighting gangs just knocked down the tops of curtain walls and blew up one corner of the strongest buildings. This was done to at least 150 castles.

1 Using the evidence of the ruins, make a sketch to show where you think the main buildings, walls and towers were.

3 The buildings and defences of Corfe Castle were in good repair when it was besieged in 1643. Later it was slighted and looks like this today.

4 Belvoir Castle was built in the nineteenth century on the place where a Norman castle was completely demolished after the Civil War.

2 How would you explain to a friend that this is not a true castle?

After the Civil War

The Civil War was the last time that most castles were used in wars. One or two were taken over by the army. For example, Dover Castle became an important fort and explosives store. Many were turned into gaols. Most of the rest were allowed to fall into even greater ruin.

Then in the nineteenth century some wealthy people began to think that a castle was a romantic place to live in. King George III took the lead by having most of Windsor Castle rebuilt. The owners of castles like Warwick, Arundel and Alnwick followed his example. The builders thought they were copying the styles of the middle ages but they were really building castles as they imagined they should be. There were even some new 'castles' built.

Cathedrals

Sad times for cathedrals

In the 1540s and 1550s the Christian Church in England broke away from the Catholic Church headed by the Pope. The first sign of this great change came when King Henry VIII ordered all monasteries to close and hand over their wealth to him.

Most monasteries quickly became ruins. In the countryside you can still see the remains of most of the buildings. Town monasteries round cathedrals like Canterbury, Chester or Winchester or round abbey churches like St Albans were often cleared away altogether apart from some of the cloisters. A few of their buildings may have been turned into private homes, storehouses or prisons.

Then the attack turned on to the things which the new rulers of the Church believed kept superstition alive. Orders went out to destroy shrines and statues and to close down chantries.

The men who carried out the royal orders went to work in the roughest way possible. At Canterbury they broke the shrine of Thomas Becket, scattered his bones and took away so much gold, silver and jewels that sixteen men were needed to carry the chests. The same thing happened to St Hugh's shrine at Lincoln and all the other shrines.

The destruction was even worse in the Civil War which began in 1642. Parliament was led by puritans who believed that God must be worshipped without fine decorations or beautiful objects. They looked on pictures, statues and even crosses as signs of idol worship. Some cathedrals were used as barracks or stables. Soldiers damaged or destroyed statues, tombs, and rood screens. They whitewashed over wall pictures to make the cathedrals as plain as possible.

After the Civil War many cathedrals remained neglected for a very long time. Most were patched up just to keep the rain out. Often the only services were for just a few people worshipping in one small part.

A description of Ely Cathedral:

. . . children are sent to play on wet days, coal carts were taken along the nave floor . . . a Farrier's [blacksmith's] forge occupied the Baptistry and pigeons were bred and shot in the Cathedral.

James Essex, an architect, writing in about 1750

1 **What does this tell you about a) the beliefs of puritans, and b) why many churches look different today from the way they did in the middle ages?**

5 **Soldiers at work in a church in the 1640s.**

Restoration

Cathedrals today have had 200 years of neglect followed by 200 years of restoration. Restoration started when Gothic came back into fashion in the 1800s. Because Gothic styles were used it is easy to believe that the buildings look just as they did in the middle ages. But that is not always so. Sometimes Victorian architects tried to improve on the work of master masons.

You can see evidence of this at St Albans. After the Civil War, the Lady Chapel in the east end of the abbey was turned into a school. By the 1870s the tower was in danger of collapse, the nave had lost much of its roof and stones were beginning to fall from its walls.

Then restoration began. The tower was strengthened and the nave and west front needed repair – but how? The matter was decided by Lord Grimthorpe who paid for most of the work. He believed the nave was in the 'wrong' styles. It was a mixture of Norman, decorated and perpendicular. The abbey ended up with what Grimthorpe thought was the 'right' style.

6 St Albans Abbey church in the 1870s.

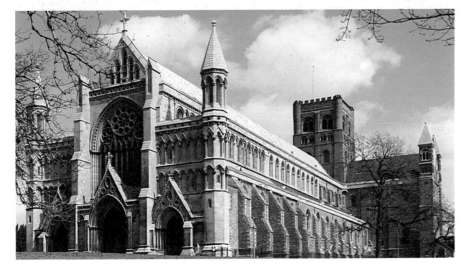

7 St Albans as it looks today.

2 List the changes which Grimthorpe had made.
3 Do you think it would have been better to have repaired the church in its old styles?
4 What clues are there that most of the outside of St Albans is just over a hundred years old.

Cathedrals and dioceses today

While it was being restored St Alban's Abbey became a cathedral. This fact reminds us that the number of bishops and dioceses has grown over the centuries. When Henry VIII became king in 1509 there were twenty-two dioceses. After he had closed the monasteries he had five abbey churches turned into cathedrals: Bristol, Chester, Oxford, Gloucester and Peterborough. In the nineteenth and twentieth centuries the number of Church of England dioceses has risen to forty-two. Three of these newest cathedrals were also once abbey churches: St Albans, Ripon and Southwark. Most of the other cathedrals were parish churches before they became the centre of a diocese, but four new ones have been built in the last hundred years. Coventry has a new cathedral linked to the ruins of its medieval building which was destroyed by war-time air-raids. Truro, Guildford and Liverpool have Church of England cathedrals built in Gothic styles.

Liverpool also has a Roman Catholic cathedral, a circular building in modern materials. But it is not the only city with two cathedrals. The Roman Catholic Church remained outlawed from Henry VIII's days until the middle of the nineteenth century. Today it has an archbishop, twenty-two dioceses and cathedrals in England and Wales, and eight in Scotland – all built in not much more than a hundred years.

8 The inside of Liverpool Roman Catholic Cathedral.

Do you think a priest who served in a cathedral in the middle ages would have approved or disapproved of this building, built to the glory of God in the twentieth century? Why?